Houghton
Mifflin
Harcourt

CALIFORNIA

MATH

Expressions
Common Core

Dr. Karen C. Fuson

GRADE

1

Volume 1

This material is based upon work supported by the
National Science Foundation
under Grant Numbers
ESI-9816320, REC-9806020, and RED-935373.

Any opinions, findings, and conclusions, or recommendations expressed in this material
are those of the author and do not necessarily reflect the views of the National Science Foundation.

VOLUME 1 CONTENTS

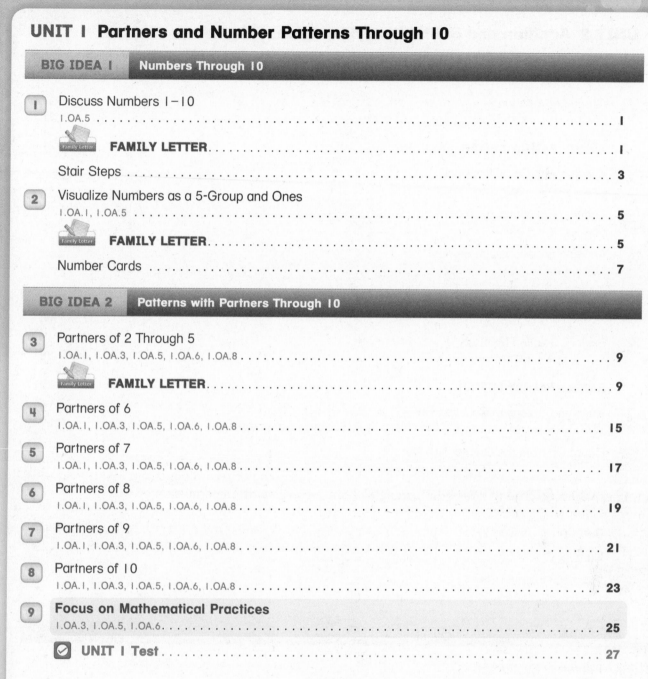

VOLUME 1 CONTENTS *(continued)*

UNIT 2 Addition and Subtraction Strategies

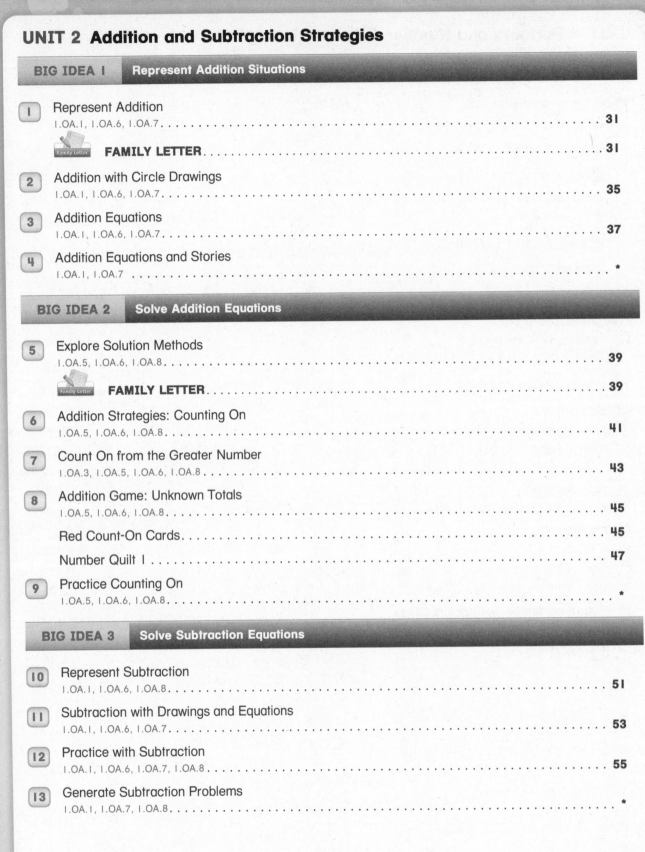
***** This lesson consists only of activities from the Teacher Edition.

© Houghton Mifflin Harcourt Publishing Company

***** This lesson consists only of activities from the Teacher Edition.

* This lesson consists only of activities from the Teacher Edition.

Student Resources

* This lesson consists only of activities from the Teacher Edition.

© Houghton Mifflin Harcourt Publishing Company

Family Letter

Content Overview

Dear Family:

Your child is learning math in an innovative program that interweaves abstract mathematical concepts with the everyday experiences of children. This helps children to understand math better.

In this program, your child will learn math and have fun by:

- working with objects and making drawings of math situations;
- working with other children and sharing problem solving strategies with them;
- writing and solving problems and connecting math to daily life;
- helping classmates learn.

Your child will have homework almost every day. He or she needs a **Homework Helper.** The helper may be anyone—you, an older brother or sister (or other family member), a neighbor, or a friend. Make a specific time for homework and provide your child with a quiet place to work (for example, no TV). Encourage your child to talk about what is happening in math class. If your child is having problems with math, please talk to me to see how you might help.

Thank you. You are vital to your child's learning.

Sincerely,
Your child's teacher

CA CC

Unit 1 addresses the following standards from the *Common Core State Standards for Mathematics with California Additions*: **1.OA.1, 1.OA.3, 1.OA.5, 1.OA.6, 1.OA.8** and all Mathematical Practices.

Please fill out the following information and return this form to the teacher.

My child _____ will have _____
                (child's name)   (Homework Helper's name)

as his or her Homework Helper. This person is my

child's _____.
        (relationship to child)

Carta a la familia

Un vistazo general al contenido

Estimada familia:

Su niño está aprendiendo matemáticas con un programa innovador que relaciona conceptos matemáticos abstractos con la experiencia diaria de los niños. Esto ayuda a los niños a entender mejor las matemáticas.

Con este programa, su niño aprenderá matemáticas y se divertirá mientras:

- trabaja con objetos y hace dibujos de problemas matemáticos;
- trabaja con otros niños y comparte estrategias para resolver problemas;
- escribe y resuelve problemas y relaciona las matemáticas con la vida diaria;
- ayuda a sus compañeros a aprender.

Su niño tendrá tarea casi todos los días y necesita a una persona que lo ayude con la tarea. Esa persona puede ser usted, un hermano mayor (u otro familiar), un vecino o un amigo. Establezca una hora para la tarea y ofrezca a su niño un lugar tranquilo donde trabajar (por ejemplo un lugar sin TV). Anime a su niño a comentar lo que está aprendiendo en la clase de matemáticas. Si su niño tiene problemas con las matemáticas, por favor comuníquese conmigo para indicarle cómo puede ayudarlo.

Muchas gracias. Usted es imprescindible en el aprendizaje de su niño.

Atentamente,
El maestro de su niño

CA CC

En la Unidad 1 se aplican los siguientes estándares auxiliares, contenidos en los *Estándares estatales comunes de matemáticas con adiciones para California*: **1.0A.1, 1.0A.3, 1.0A.5, 1.0A.6, 1.0A.8** y todos los de prácticas matemáticas.

Por favor complete la siguiente información y devuelva este formulario al maestro.

La persona que ayudará a mi niño _____ es
                                         (nombre del niño)

_____. Esta persona es _____
(nombre de la persona)   (relación con el niño)

de mi niño.

© Houghton Mifflin Harcourt Publishing Company

Discuss Numbers I–I0

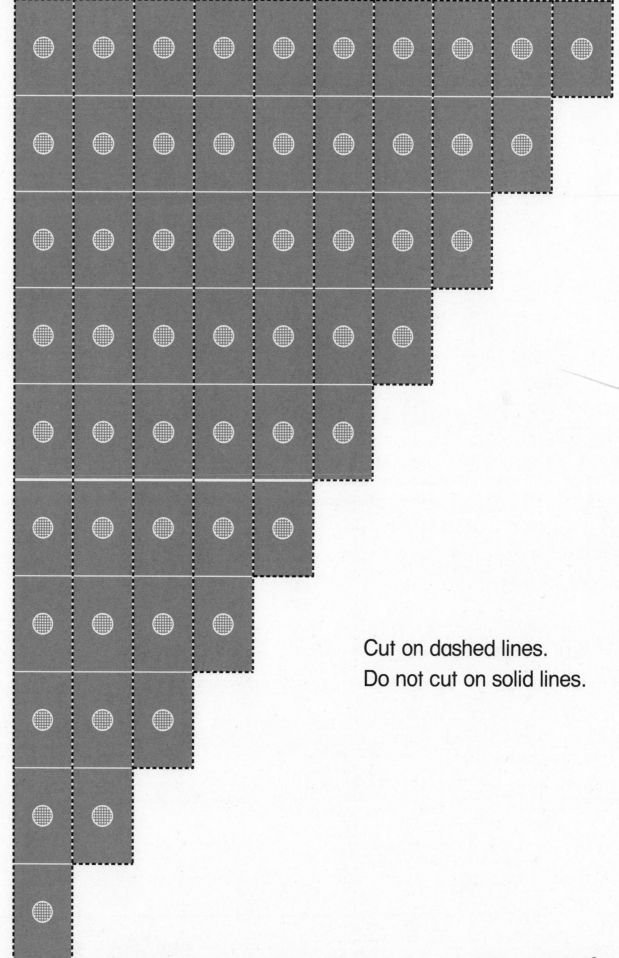

Cut on dashed lines.
Do not cut on solid lines.

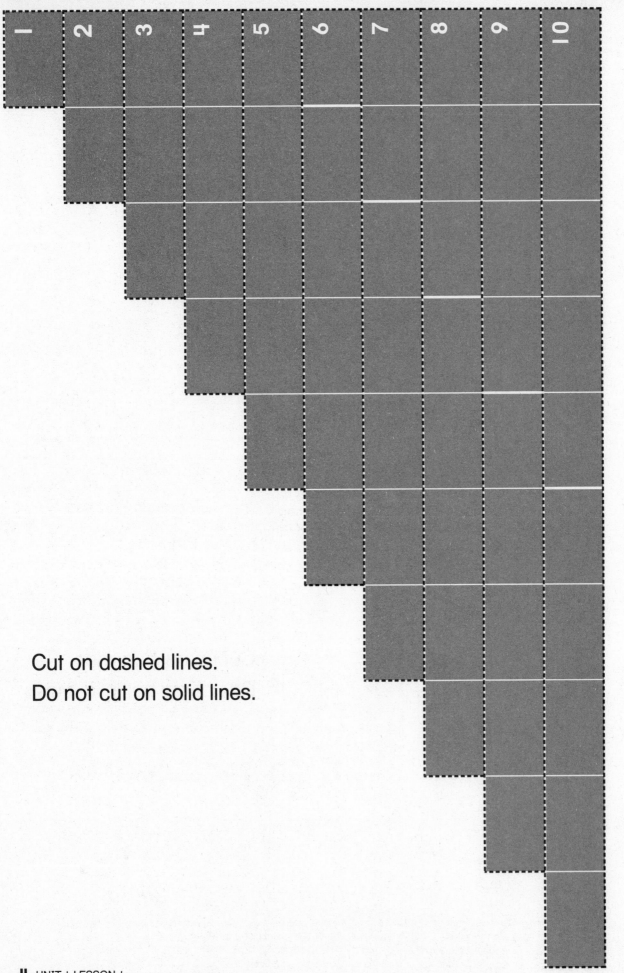

Cut on dashed lines.
Do not cut on solid lines.

Family Letter

Content Overview

Dear Family:

Your child is learning to see numbers as a group of 5 and extra ones. Making mental pictures by grouping units in this way will later help your child add and subtract quickly. Children benefit greatly from learning to "see" numbers without counting every unit.

Children start exploring these 5-groups by looking at dots arranged in a row of 5 plus some extra ones. Below are samples that show the numbers from 6 through 10.

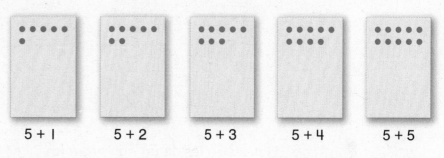

5 + 1   5 + 2   5 + 3   5 + 4   5 + 5

The teacher gives the children a number and asks them to say it as a 5 plus extra ones. Children say the numbers in order at first. Later they can "see" the quantities even when the numbers are shown randomly.

Teacher: What is 6?

Class: 5 + 1

Teacher: What is 7?

Class: 5 + 2

On some homework pages, you will find instructions that ask children to "see the 5." Your child is being encouraged to make a mental picture of a number that contains a 5-group. Later, the children will be asked to see groups of 10 by combining two 5-groups. This will help them learn place value.

It takes repeated exposure to such groups for children to see the numbers quickly. Many of the visual aids in your child's classroom include 5-groups. Children tend to absorb these visual patterns without realizing it.

If you have any questions or problems, please contact me.

Sincerely,
Your child's teacher

 CA CC

Unit 1 addresses the following standards from the *Common Core State Standards for Mathematics with California Additions*: **1.OA.1, 1.OA.3, 1.OA.5, 1.OA.6, 1.OA.8** and all Mathematical Practices.

Visualize Numbers as a 5-Group and Ones **5**

Estimada familia:

Su niño está aprendiendo a ver los números como un grupo de 5 más otras unidades. El hecho de agrupar mentalmente unidades de esa manera ayudará a su niño a sumar y restar rápidamente en el futuro. Los niños se benefician muchísimo de aprender a "ver" los números sin contar cada unidad.

Los niños comienzan a practicar con estos grupos de 5 observando puntos distribuidos en una fila de 5 más otras unidades. Estos ejemplos muestran los números del 6 al 10.

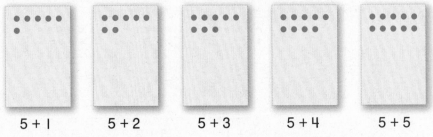

5 + 1   5 + 2   5 + 3   5 + 4   5 + 5

El maestro les da un número a los niños y les pide que lo digan como 5 más otras unidades. Al principio, los niños dicen los números en orden. Más adelante pueden "ver" las cantidades incluso cuando los números se muestran sin un orden específico.

Maestro: ¿Qué es el 6?

Clase: 5 + 1

Maestro: ¿Qué es el 7?

Clase: 5 + 2

En algunas páginas de tarea hallará instrucciones que piden a los niños "ver el número 5". A su niño se le está animando a que visualice un número que contenga un grupo de 5. Más adelante, se les pedirá que vean grupos de 10, combinando dos grupos de 5. Esto les ayudará a aprender el valor posicional.

Es necesario que los niños practiquen muchas veces los grupos de este tipo para que puedan llegar a ver los números rápidamente. Muchas de las ayudas visuales que hay en el salón de clase incluyen grupos de 5. Los niños tienden a absorber estos patrones visuales sin darse cuenta.

Si tiene alguna pregunta o algún comentario, por favor comuníquese conmigo.

Atentamente,
El maestro de su niño

© Houghton Mifflin Harcourt Publishing Company

 CA CC

En la Unidad 1 se aplican los siguientes estándares auxiliares, contenidos en los *Estándares estatales comunes de matemáticas con adiciones para California*: **1.OA.1, 1.OA.3, 1.OA.5, 1.OA.6, 1.OA.8** y todos los de prácticas matemáticas.

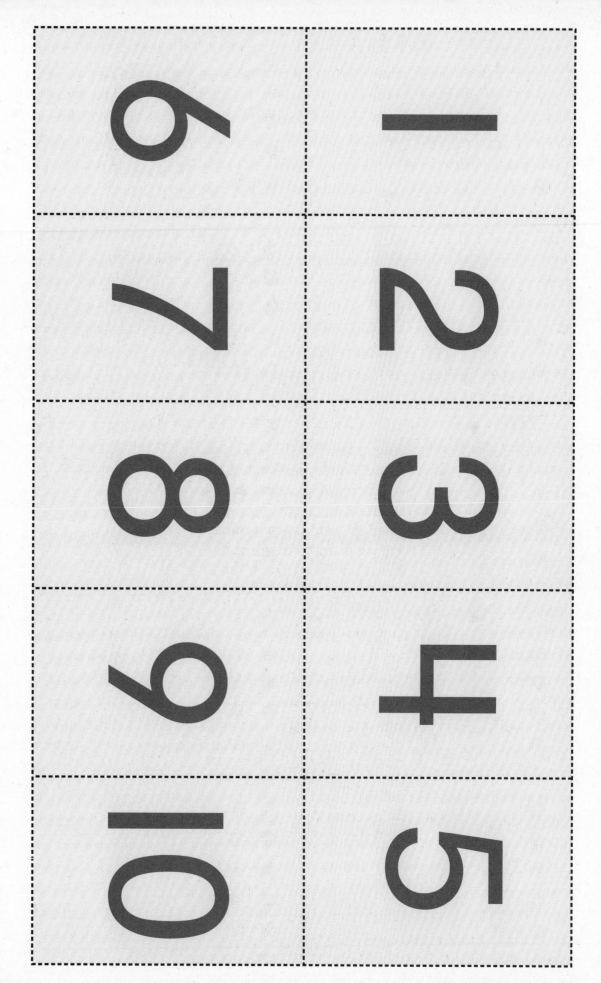

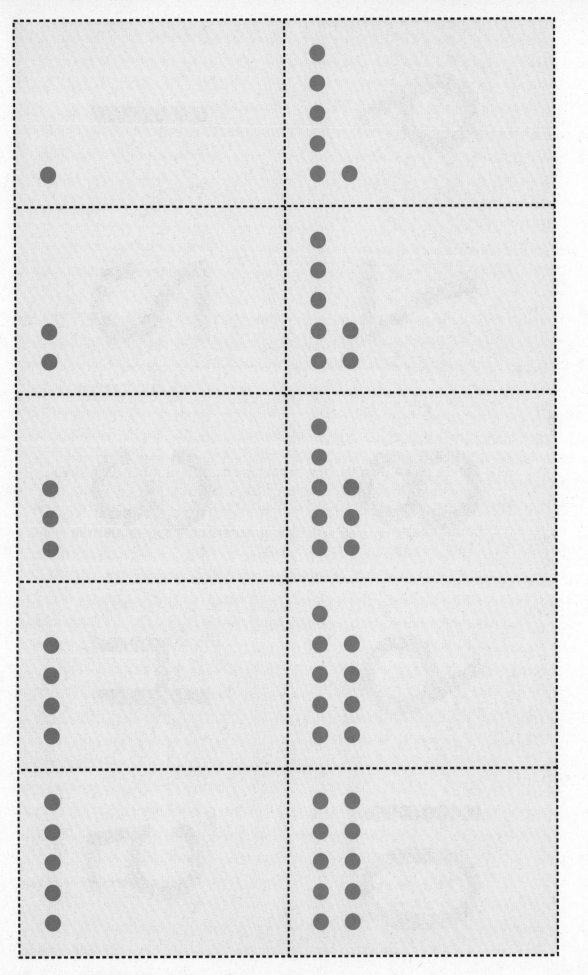

Family Letter

Content Overview

Dear Family:

Your child is learning to find the smaller numbers that are "hiding" inside a larger number. He or she will be participating in activities that will help him or her master addition, subtraction, and equation building.

To make the concepts clear, this program uses some special vocabulary and materials that we would like to share. Below are two important terms that your child is learning:

- **Partners:** Partners are two numbers that can be put together to make a larger number. For example, 2 and 5 are partners that go together to make the number 7.

- **Break Apart:** Children can "break apart" a larger number to form two smaller numbers. Your child is using objects and drawings to explore ways of "breaking apart" numbers of ten or less.

Partners of 7

Children can discover the break-aparts of a number with circle drawings. They first draw the "Break-Apart Stick" and then color the circles to show the different partners, as shown below. Sometimes they also write the partners on a special partner train, which is also shown below.

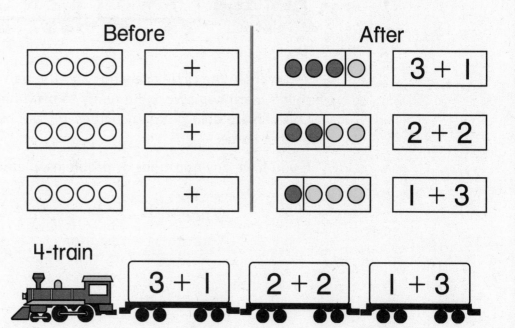

Later, children will discover that partners can change places without changing the total. This concept is called "switch the partners." Once children understand switching partners, they can find the break-aparts of a number more quickly. They simply switch each pair of partners as they discover them.

Shown below are the break-aparts and switched partners of the number 7. Sometimes children also write this information on a double-decker train.

Break-Aparts of 7

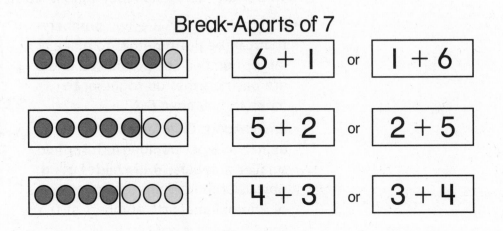

Double-Decker Train

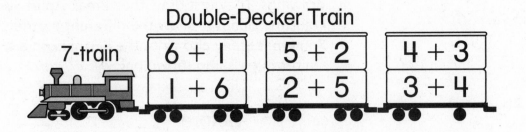

You will see the circle drawings and the partner trains on your child's math homework. Be ready to offer help if it is needed. Children are doing these activities in class, but they may still need help at home.

If you have any questions or problems, please talk to me.

Sincerely,
Your child's teacher

© Houghton Mifflin Harcourt Publishing Company

CA CC

Unit 1 addresses the following standards from the *Common Core State Standards for Mathematics with California Additions*: **1.OA.1, 1.OA.3, 1.OA.5, 1.OA.6, 1.OA.8** and all Mathematical Practices.

Partners of 2 Through 5

Un vistazo general al contenido

Estimada familia:

Su niño está aprendiendo a hallar los números más pequeños que están "escondidos" dentro de un número más grande. Va a participar en actividades que le ayudarán a dominar la suma, la resta y la formación de ecuaciones.

Para clarificar los conceptos, este programa usa un vocabulario especial y algunos materiales que nos gustaría mostrarle. A continuación hay dos términos importantes que su niño está aprendiendo:

- **Partes:** Partes son dos números que se pueden unir para formar un número más grande. Por ejemplo, 2 y 5 son partes que se unen para formar el número 7.

- **Separar:** Los niños pueden "separar" un número más grande para formar dos números más pequeños. Su niño está usando objetos y dibujos para explorar maneras de "separar" números iguales o menores que diez.

Partes de 7

Los niños pueden separar un número usando dibujos de círculos. Primero dibujan un "palito de separación" y luego colorean los círculos para indicar las partes, como se muestra a continuación. A veces los niños anotan las partes en un tren de partes especial, que también se muestra a continuación.

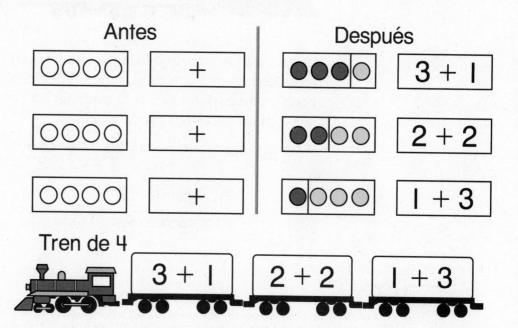

Antes | Después

○○○○ | + | ●●●○ | 3 + 1

○○○○ | + | ●●○○ | 2 + 2

○○○○ | + | ●○○○ | 1 + 3

Tren de 4

3 + 1   2 + 2   1 + 3

Luego, los niños van a aprender que las partes pueden intercambiar su posición sin que varíe el total. Este concepto se llama "cambiar el orden de las partes". Una vez que los niños entienden el cambio del orden de las partes, pueden encontrar las partes de un número con más rapidez. Sencillamente cambian cada par de partes a medida que las encuentran.

A continuación están las partes, y las partes en otro orden, del número 7. A veces los niños escriben esta información en un tren de dos pisos.

Partes de 7

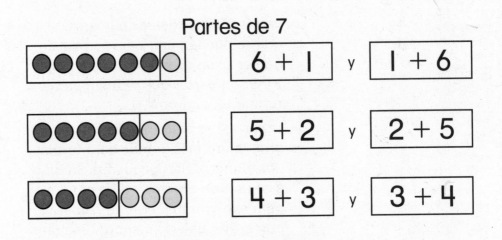

Tren de 7

Tren de dos pisos

Usted verá los dibujos de los círculos y los trenes de partes en la tarea de matemáticas de su niño. Ayúdelo, si es necesario. Los niños están haciendo estas actividades en clase, pero es posible que aún así necesiten ayuda en casa.

Si tiene preguntas o dudas, por favor comuníquese conmigo.

Atentamente,
El maestro de su niño

© Houghton Mifflin Harcourt Publishing Company

 CA CC

En la Unidad 1 se aplican los siguientes estándares auxiliares, contenidos en los *Estándares estatales comunes de matemáticas con adiciones para California*: **1.OA.1, 1.OA.3, 1.OA.5, 1.OA.6, 1.OA.8** y todos los de prácticas matemáticas.

Partners of 2 Through 5

Name _____

CA CC Content Standards 1.OA.3, 1.OA.5, 1.OA.6,
1.OA.8 Mathematical Practices MP.1, MP.2, MP.7, MP.8

Show the 8-partners and switch the partners.

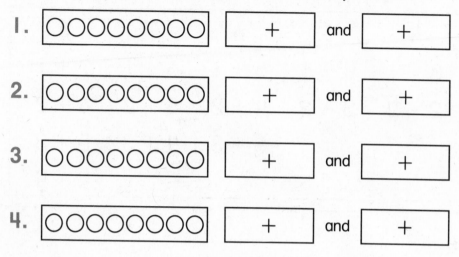

1. ⊂OOOOOOOO⊃ ☐ + ☐ and ☐ + ☐

2. ⊂OOOOOOOO⊃ ☐ + ☐ and ☐ + ☐

3. ⊂OOOOOOOO⊃ ☐ + ☐ and ☐ + ☐

4. ⊂OOOOOOOO⊃ ☐ + ☐ and ☐ + ☐

Write the partners and the switched partners.

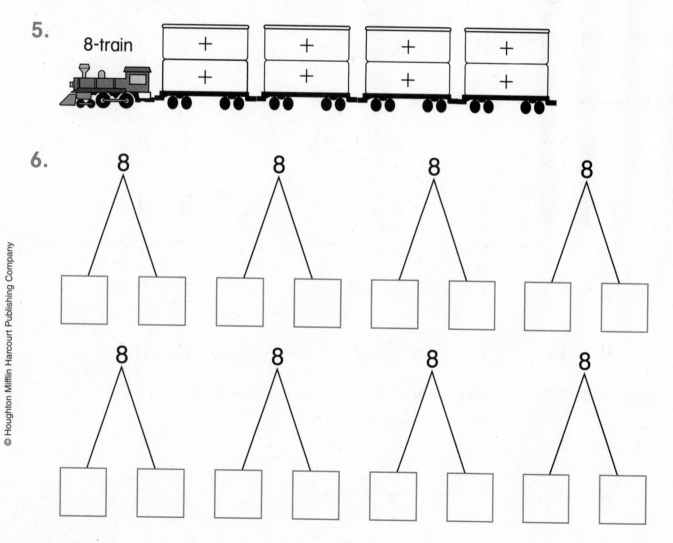

5. 8-train

☐ + ☐   ☐ + ☐   ☐ + ☐   ☐ + ☐
☐ + ☐   ☐ + ☐   ☐ + ☐   ☐ + ☐

6.   8   8   8   8
    ☐ ☐   ☐ ☐   ☐ ☐   ☐ ☐

      8   8   8   8
    ☐ ☐   ☐ ☐   ☐ ☐   ☐ ☐

Name _____

7. Discuss patterns in the partners.

2	3	4	5	6	7	8
1 + 1	2 + 1	3 + 1	4 + 1	5 + 1	6 + 1	7 + 1
		2 + 2	3 + 2	4 + 2	5 + 2	6 + 2
			3 + 3	4 + 3	5 + 3	
				4 + 4		

Use doubles to solve.

8. $4 + 4 =$ ☐ $3 + 3 =$ ☐ $2 + 2 =$ ☐

 $8 - 4 =$ ☐ $6 - 3 =$ ☐ $4 - 2 =$ ☐

Use patterns to solve.

9. $8 + 0 =$ ☐ $6 + 0 =$ ☐ $7 + 0 =$ ☐

 $0 + 5 =$ ☐ $0 + 3 =$ ☐ $0 + 4 =$ ☐

10. $7 - 0 =$ ☐ $2 - 0 =$ ☐ $8 - 0 =$ ☐

 $5 - 0 =$ ☐ $3 - 0 =$ ☐ $6 - 0 =$ ☐

11. $4 - 4 =$ ☐ $6 - 6 =$ ☐ $2 - 2 =$ ☐

 $8 - 8 =$ ☐ $7 - 7 =$ ☐ $5 - 5 =$ ☐

Partners of 8

Name

CA CC Content Standards **1.0A.3, 1.0A.5, 1.0A.6, 1.0A.8** Mathematical Practices **MP.2, MP.7, MP.8**

Show the 9-partners and switch the partners.

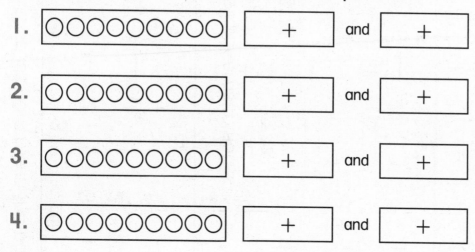

1. ◯◯◯◯◯◯◯◯◯ [+] and [+]

2. ◯◯◯◯◯◯◯◯◯ [+] and [+]

3. ◯◯◯◯◯◯◯◯◯ [+] and [+]

4. ◯◯◯◯◯◯◯◯◯ [+] and [+]

Write the partners and the switched partners.

5.

9-train

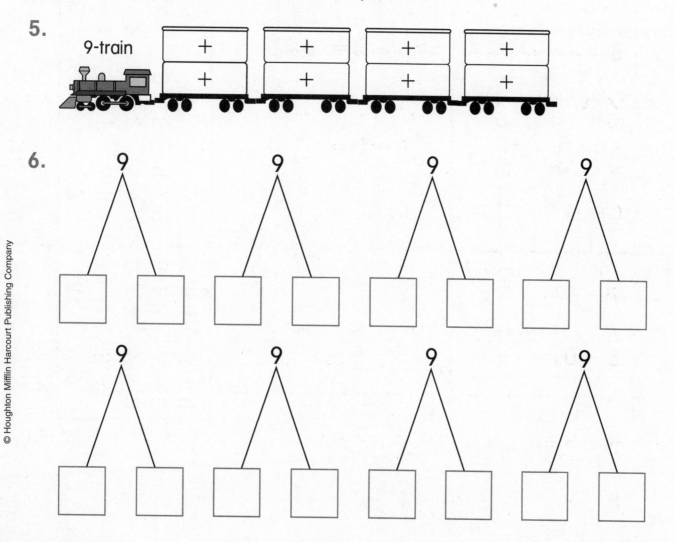

6.

Name

7. Discuss patterns in the partners.

2	**3**	**4**	**5**	**6**	**7**	**8**	**9**
1 + 1	2 + 1	3 + 1	4 + 1	5 + 1	6 + 1	7 + 1	8 + 1
	2 + 2	3 + 2	4 + 2	5 + 2	6 + 2	7 + 2	
		3 + 3	4 + 3	5 + 3	6 + 3	7 + 3	
			4 + 4	5 + 4	6 + 4	5 + 4	

Use patterns to solve.

8. 6 + 1 = ☐   8 + 1 = ☐

   4 + 1 = ☐   3 + 1 = ☐

   5 + 1 = ☐   7 + 1 = ☐

9. 1 + 7 = ☐   1 + 2 = ☐

   1 + 8 = ☐   1 + 4 = ☐

   1 + 6 = ☐   1 + 5 = ☐

10. 9 − 1 = ☐   3 − 1 = ☐

    7 − 1 = ☐   6 − 1 = ☐

    8 − 1 = ☐   5 − 1 = ☐

11. 9 − 8 = ☐   3 − 2 = ☐

    7 − 6 = ☐   6 − 5 = ☐

    8 − 7 = ☐   5 − 4 = ☐

Name _____

CA CC Content Standards **1.OA.3, 1.OA.5, 1.OA.6, 1.OA.8** Mathematical Practices **MP.1, MP.2, MP.6, MP.7, MP.8**

1. Discuss patterns.

Partners of 10

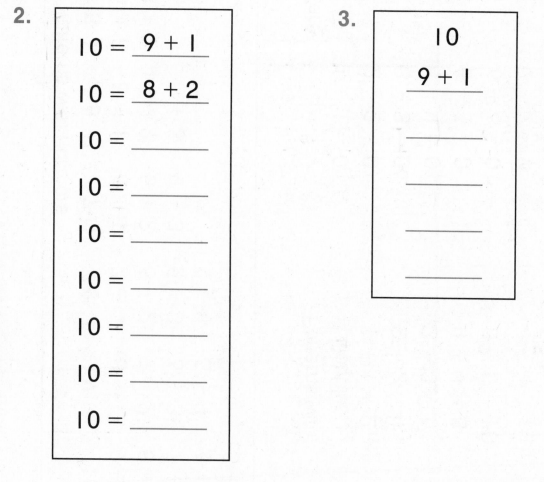

| 9 + 1 | 8 + 2 | 7 + 3 | 6 + 4 | 5 + 5 |
| 1 + 9 | 2 + 8 | 3 + 7 | 4 + 6 | |

Write the 10-partners.

2.

10 = <u>9 + 1</u>

10 = <u>8 + 2</u>

10 = _____

10 = _____

10 = _____

10 = _____

10 = _____

10 = _____

10 = _____

3.

10

<u>9 + 1</u>

_____

_____

_____

_____

4. Discuss patterns.

Patterns with Partners

2	**3**	**4**	**5**	**6**	**7**	**8**	**9**	**10**
1 + 1	2 + 1	3 + 1	4 + 1	5 + 1	6 + 1	7 + 1	8 + 1	9 + 1
		2 + 2	3 + 2	4 + 2	5 + 2	6 + 2	7 + 2	8 + 2
			3 + 3	4 + 3	5 + 3	6 + 3	7 + 3
					4 + 4	5 + 4	6 + 4	7 + 4
							5 + 5

Patterns with Zero

1 + 0 = 1	1 − 0 = 1
2 + 0 = 2	2 − 0 = 2
3 + 0 = 3	3 − 0 = 3
4 + 0 = 4	4 − 0 = 4
5 + 0 = 5	5 − 0 = 5
6 + 0 = 6	6 − 0 = 6
7 + 0 = 7	7 − 0 = 7
8 + 0 = 8	8 − 0 = 8
9 + 0 = 9	9 − 0 = 9
10 + 0 = 10	10 − 0 = 10

1 − 1 = 0
2 − 2 = 0
3 − 3 = 0
4 − 4 = 0
5 − 5 = 0
6 − 6 = 0
7 − 7 = 0
8 − 8 = 0
9 − 9 = 0
10 − 10 = 0

Patterns with Doubles

1 + 1 = 2
2 + 2 = 4
3 + 3 = 6
4 + 4 = 8
5 + 5 = 10

Name

CA CC Content Standards **1.0A.3, 1.0A.5, 1.0A.6** Mathematical Practices **MP.1, MP.4, MP.5**

▶ Math and a Marching Band

Write the number of band members in each row.

1.

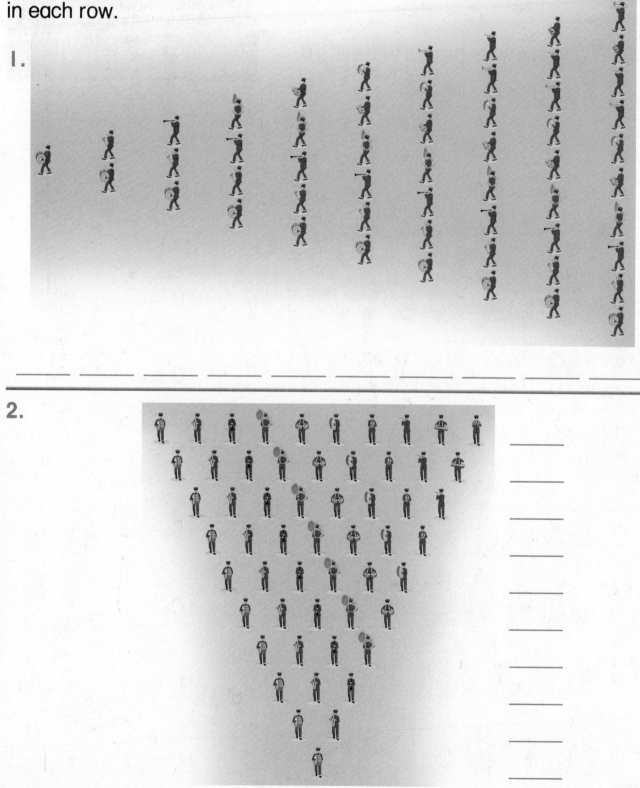

2.

Name _____

3. Show and write the partners of 10.

$10 = \underline{5} + \underline{5}$

$10 = \underline{7} + \underline{3}$

$10 = \underline{3} + \underline{7}$

$10 = \underline{10} + \underline{0}$

$10 = \underline{3} + \underline{7}$

$10 = \underline{3} + \underline{7}$

$10 = \underline{1} + \underline{9}$

$10 = \underline{8} + \underline{2}$

$10 = \underline{3} + \underline{7}$

Focus on Mathematical Practices

See the 5-group.
Draw extra dots to show the number.

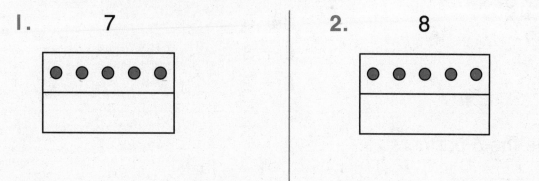

1. 7

2. 8

3. Does the picture match the number?
   Choose Yes or No.

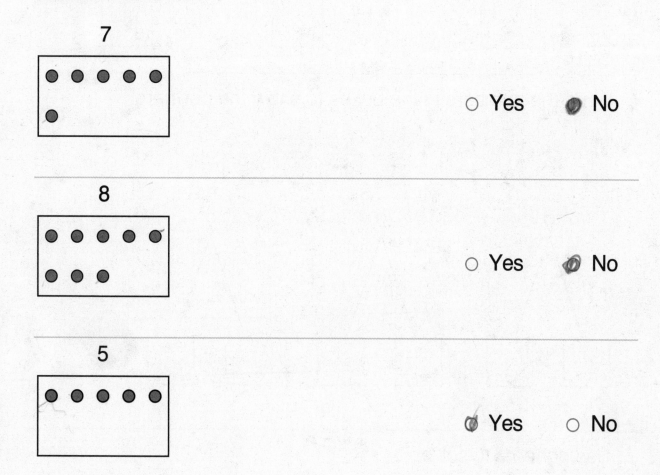

7

○ Yes   ● No

8

○ Yes   ● No

5

● Yes   ○ No

Choose all the 10-partners.

4. ●●●●●
   ●●●○○

   ○ 2 + 8
   ○ 3 + 5
   ○ 8 + 3
   ○ 8 + 2

5. Complete the 6-partners.

$$6 = 5 + \begin{array}{|c|} \hline 1 \\ 2 \\ 3 \\ \hline \end{array}$$
$$6 = 4 + \begin{array}{|c|} \hline 0 \\ 1 \\ 2 \\ \hline \end{array}$$
$$6 = \begin{array}{|c|} \hline 0 \\ 1 \\ 2 \\ \hline \end{array} + 6$$

6. Write the numbers in the boxes to show the partners.

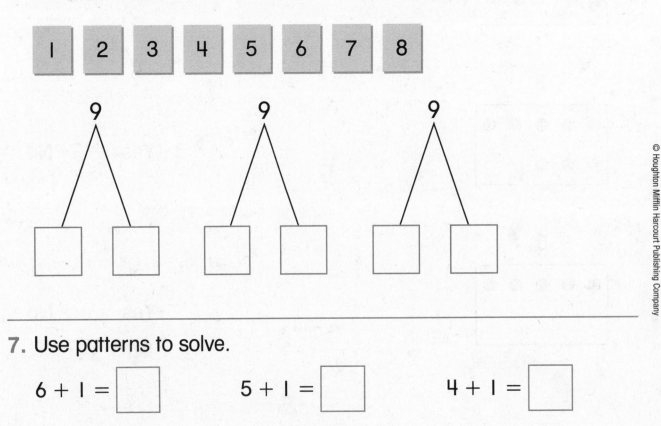

1 2 3 4 5 6 7 8

7. Use patterns to solve.

6 + 1 = ☐   5 + 1 = ☐   4 + 1 = ☐

Write the partners.

8.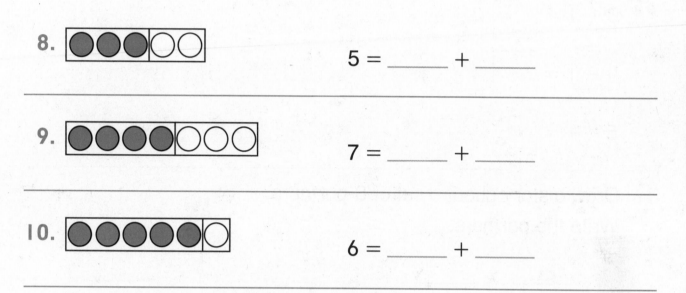

5 = _____ + _____

9.

7 = _____ + _____

10.

6 = _____ + _____

11. Write facts that match each total.

| 8 + 1 | 9 + 0 | 6 + 1 | 4 + 4 | 7 + 0 | 1 + 7 |

7	8	9

Write the partners and the switched partners.

12.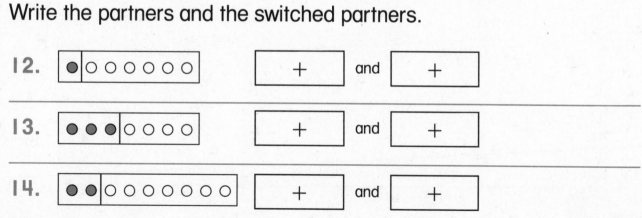

____ + ____ and ____ + ____

13.

____ + ____ and ____ + ____

14.

____ + ____ and ____ + ____

15. Use patterns to solve.

3 − 1 = ☐

4 − 1 = ☐

5 − 1 = ☐

16. Draw a story about a set of 8-partners.
Write the partners.

Dear Family:

Your child has started a new unit on addition, subtraction, and equations. These concepts are introduced with stories that capture children's interest and help them to see adding and subtracting as real-life processes.

At the beginning of the unit, children show a story problem by drawing a picture of the objects. If they are adding 4 balloons and 2 balloons, for example, their pictures might look like the top one shown here. If they are subtracting, their pictures might look like the bottom one.

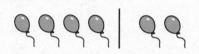

Addition

Subtraction

In a short time, children will show objects quickly with circles rather than pictures. This is a major conceptual advance because it requires the use of symbols. Children are asked to show the partners (4 + 2) as well as give the total (6). From here, children are just a small step away from writing standard equations, such as $4 + 2 = 6$ and $6 - 4 = 2$.

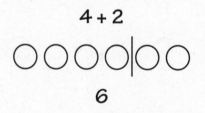

4 + 2

6

Addition Problem

6 − 4

2

Subtraction Problem

To keep them focused on the actual problem, children are often asked to give a "complete answer" in class. This means that they should name the objects as well as give the number. Right now, complete answers are not required for homework. Even so, it would be helpful for you to ask your child to say the complete answer when working with you at home. Example: "You said the answer is 6. Is it 6 dinosaurs? No? Then 6 what? . . . Oh! 6 balloons!"

Sincerely,
Your child's teacher

CA CC

Unit 2 addresses the following standards from the *Common Core State Standards for Mathematics with California Additions*: **1.OA.1, 1.OA.3, 1.OA.5, 1.OA.6, 1.OA.7, 1.OA.8** and all Mathematical Practices.

Carta a la familia

Un vistazo general al contenido

Estimada familia:

Su niño ha empezado una nueva unidad sobre la suma, la resta y las ecuaciones. Estos conceptos se presentan con cuentos que captan el interés de los niños y les ayudan a ver la suma y la resta como procesos de la vida diaria.

Al comienzo de la unidad, los niños muestran un problema en forma de cuento haciendo un dibujo de los objetos. Por ejemplo, si están sumando 4 globos y 2 globos, sus dibujos pueden parecerse al dibujo de arriba. Si están restando, es posible que sus dibujos se parezcan al dibujo de abajo.

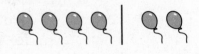

Suma

Al poco tiempo, los niños mostrarán objetos rápidamente con círculos en vez de dibujos. Esto es un gran paso conceptual, ya que requiere el uso de signos.

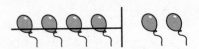

Resta

A los niños se les pide que muestren las partes (4 + 2) y la respuesta (6). Una vez que hacen esto, están casi listos para escribir ecuaciones normales, tales como $4 + 2 = 6$ y $6 - 4 = 2$.

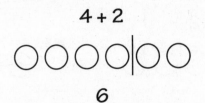

4 + 2

6

Problema de suma

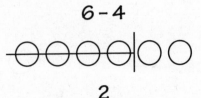

6 – 4

2

Problema de resta

Para que sigan concentrándose en el problema mismo, a los niños se les pide una "respuesta completa" en la clase. Esto significa que deben nombrar los objetos y dar el número. Actualmente, no se requieren respuestas completas en la tarea. Sin embargo, sería de ayuda si le pidiera a su niño que le dé la respuesta completa cuando trabaja con Ud. en casa. Por ejemplo: "Dijiste que la respuesta es 6. ¿Son 6 dinosaurios? ¿No? Entonces, ¿6 de qué?. . . ¡Ajá! ¡6 globos!"

Atentamente,
El maestro de su niño

 CA CC

En la Unidad 2 se aplican los siguientes estándares auxiliares, contenidos en los *Estándares estatales comunes de matemáticas con adiciones para California*: **1.OA.1, 1.OA.3, 1.OA.5, 1.OA.6, 1.OA.7, 1.OA.8** y todos los de prácticas matemáticas.

Represent Addition

Name _____

CA CC Content Standards **1.0A.6, 1.0A.7**
Mathematical Practices **MP.2**

VOCABULARY
partners
total

Write the **partners** and the **total**.

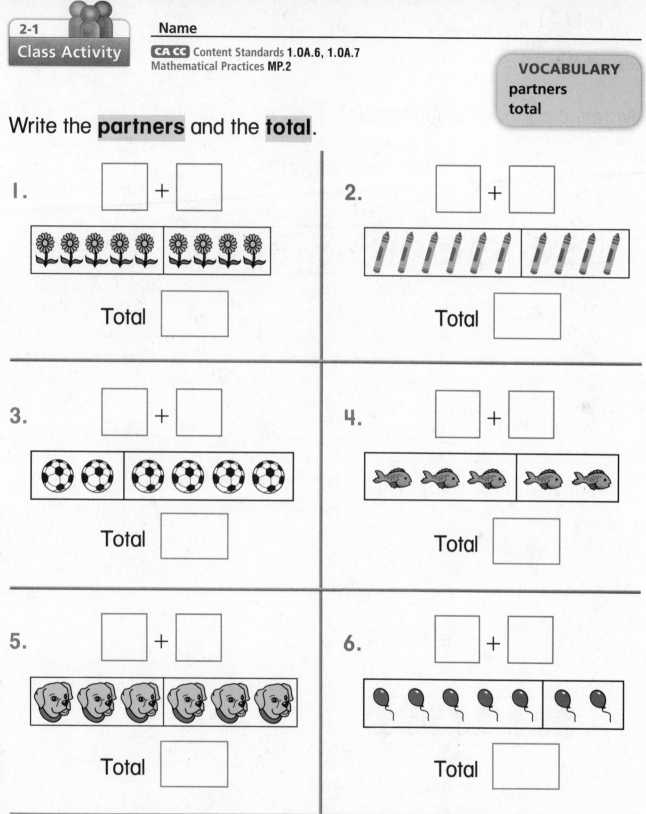

1. ☐ + ☐

   Total ☐

2. ☐ + ☐

   Total ☐

3. ☐ + ☐

   Total ☐

4. ☐ + ☐

   Total ☐

5. ☐ + ☐

   Total ☐

6. ☐ + ☐

   Total ☐

7. Draw a picture of flowers to show 4 + 2. Write the total.

Write the partners and the total.

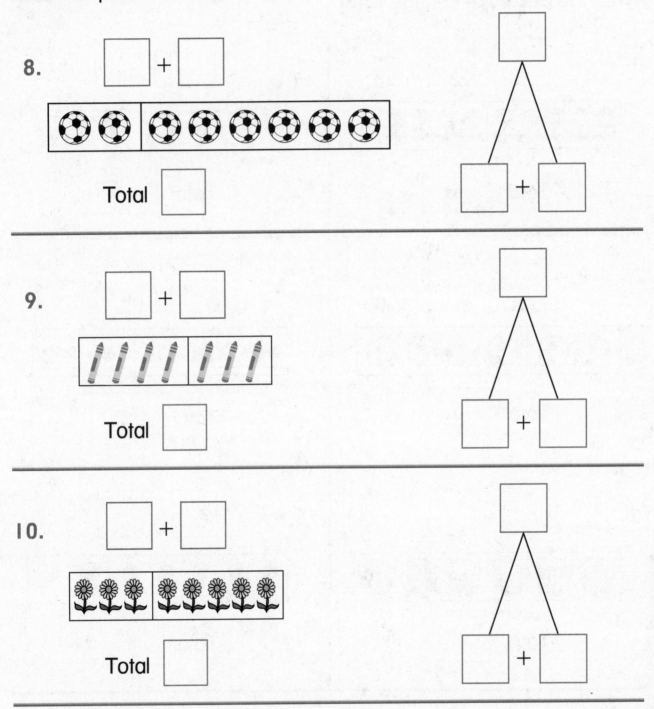

8. ☐ + ☐

Total ☐

9. ☐ + ☐

Total ☐

10. ☐ + ☐

Total ☐

11. Draw a Math Mountain to show 6 + 2.
    Write the total.

CA CC Content Standards 1.OA.6, 1.OA.7
Mathematical Practices MP.2, MP.3

VOCABULARY
circle drawing

Write the partners and total for each **circle drawing**.

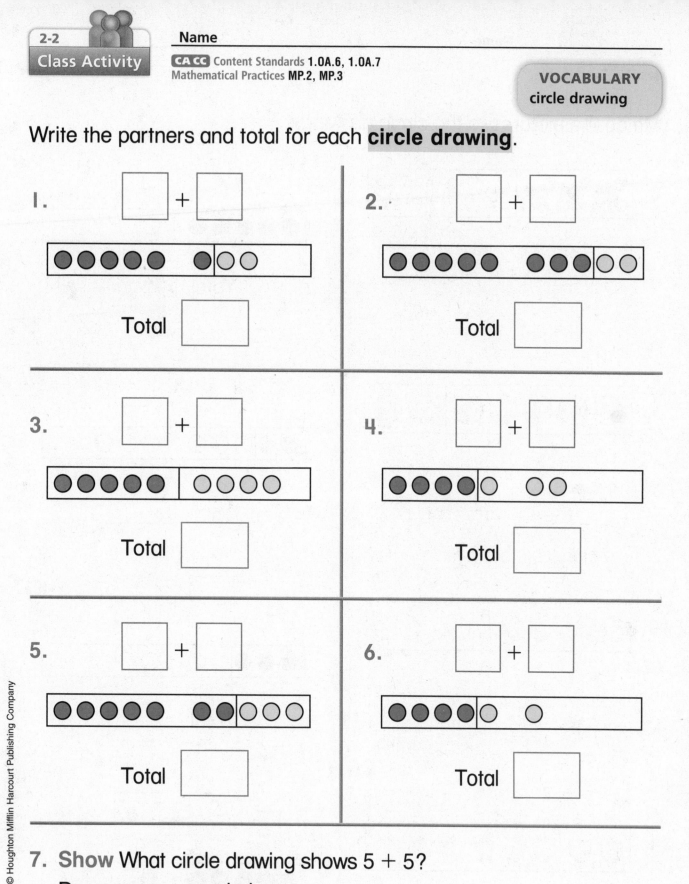

1. ☐ + ☐

Total ☐

2. ☐ + ☐

Total ☐

3. ☐ + ☐

Total ☐

4. ☐ + ☐

Total ☐

5. ☐ + ☐

Total ☐

6. ☐ + ☐

Total ☐

7. **Show** What circle drawing shows 5 + 5?
Draw your answer below.

Name

Match the pictures to the circle drawings.

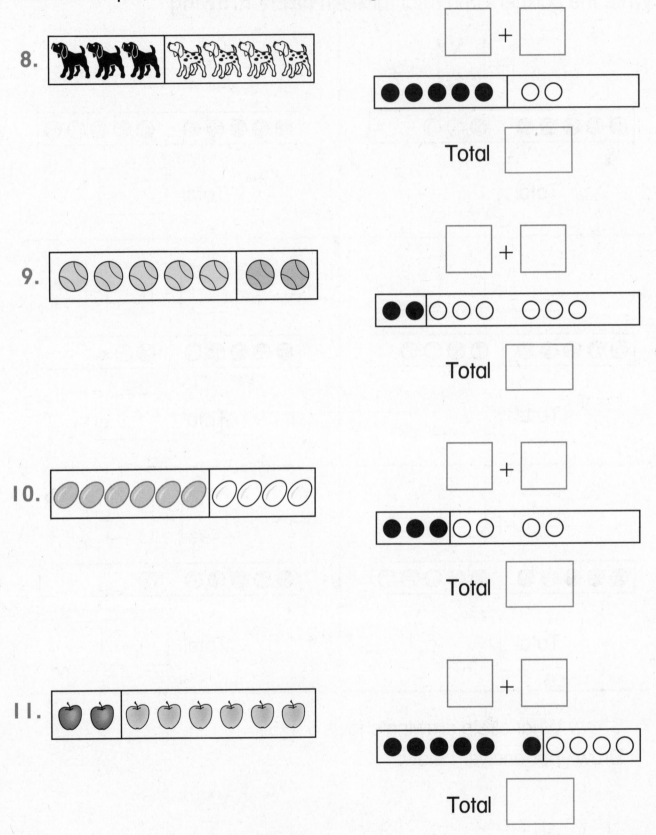

Addition with Circle Drawings

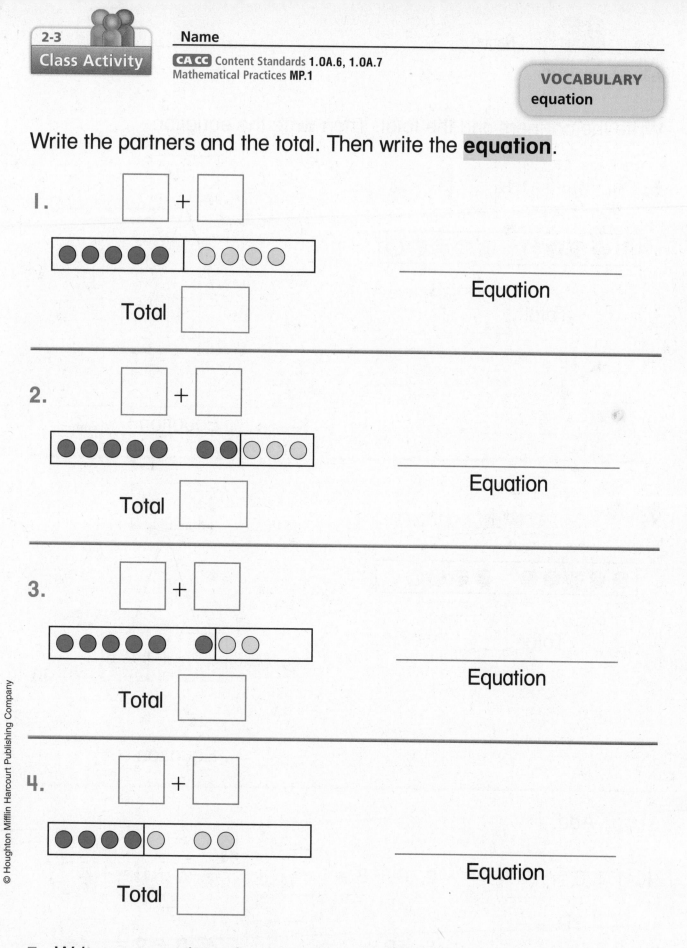

2-3
Class Activity

Name _____

CA CC Content Standards **1.0A.6, 1.0A.7**
Mathematical Practices **MP.1**

VOCABULARY
equation

Write the partners and the total. Then write the **equation**.

1. ☐ + ☐

Total ☐

_____
Equation

2. ☐ + ☐

Total ☐

_____
Equation

3. ☐ + ☐

Total ☐

_____
Equation

4. ☐ + ☐

Total ☐

_____
Equation

5. Write an equation of your own. _____

Name

Write the partners and the total. Then write the equation.

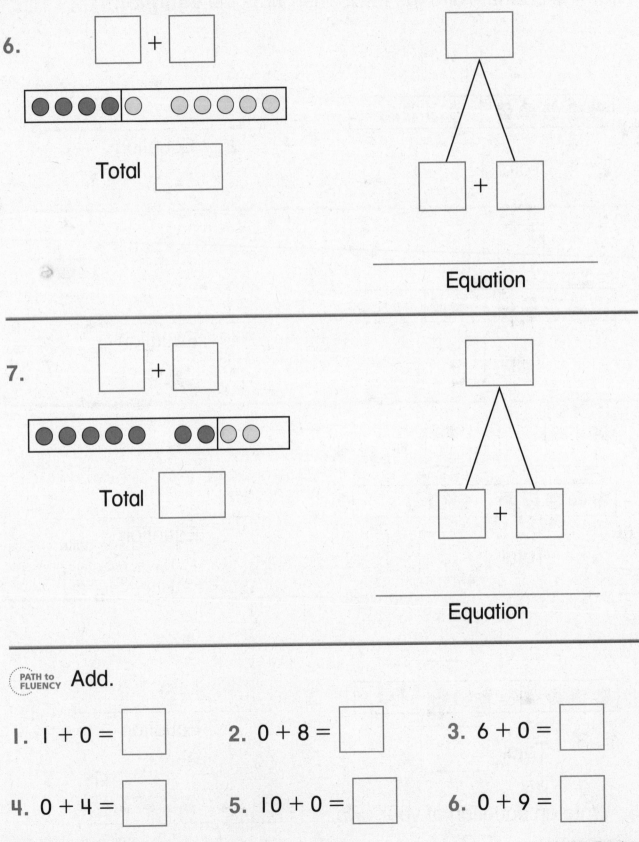

6. ☐ + ☐

Total ☐

☐
☐ + ☐

_____
Equation

7. ☐ + ☐

Total ☐

☐
☐ + ☐

_____
Equation

PATH to FLUENCY Add.

1. $1 + 0 =$ ☐

2. $0 + 8 =$ ☐

3. $6 + 0 =$ ☐

4. $0 + 4 =$ ☐

5. $10 + 0 =$ ☐

6. $0 + 9 =$ ☐

Addition Equations

Dear Family:

Earlier in the unit, your child solved addition problems by making math drawings and counting every object. This is called *counting all*. Now your child is learning a faster strategy that allows them to work directly with numbers. The method they are learning is called *counting on*. It is explained below.

In an addition problem such as 5 + 4, children say (or "think") the first number as if they had already counted it. Then they count on from there. The last number they say is the total. Children can keep track by raising a finger or making a dot for each number as they count on. The diagram below shows both the finger method and the dot method.

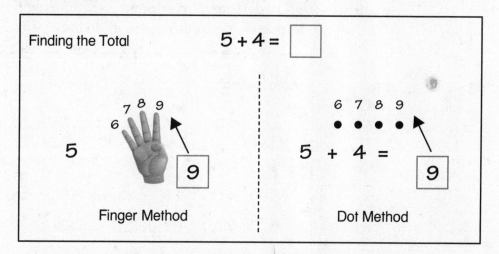

Finding the Total   5 + 4 = ☐

Finger Method   Dot Method

5 + 4 = 9

Counting on requires repeated practice. This is provided in class activities and homework assignments. Right now, your child is learning how to find unknown totals. In the next unit, he or she will learn to use the Counting On strategy to subtract.

Counting on is a temporary method to help children build fluency with addition and subtraction within 10. The goal by the end of the grade is for children to automatically know the answer when the total is 10 or less.

Sincerely,
Your child's teacher

© Houghton Mifflin Harcourt Publishing Company

 CA CC

Unit 2 addresses the following standards from the *Common Core State Standards for Mathematics with California Additions*: **1.OA.1, 1.OA.3, 1.OA.5, 1.OA.6, 1.OA.7, 1.OA.8** and all Mathematical Practices.

Estimada familia:

Un poco antes en la unidad su niño resolvió problemas de suma haciendo dibujos matemáticos y contando todos los objetos. A esto se le llama *contar todo*. Ahora su niño está aprendiendo una estrategia más rápida que le permite trabajar directamente con los números. El método que está aprendiendo se llama *contar hacia adelante*. Se explica a continuación.

En un problema de suma, como $5 + 4$, los niños dicen (o "piensan") el primer número como si ya lo hubieran contado. Luego cuentan hacia adelante a partir de él. El último número que dicen es el total. Los niños pueden llevar la cuenta levantando un dedo o haciendo un punto por cada número mientras cuentan hacia adelante. El diagrama a continuación muestra tanto el método de los dedos como el de los puntos.

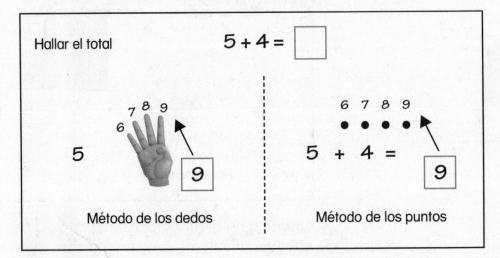

Hallar el total $5 + 4 = \boxed{}$

5   6 7 8 9 $\boxed{9}$

Método de los dedos

5 + 4 =   6 7 8 9 $\boxed{9}$

Método de los puntos

Contar hacia adelante requiere práctica. Esto sucede en las actividades de clase y tareas. En esta unidad, su niño está aprendiendo a hallar un total desconocido. En la próxima unidad, aprenderá a usar la estrategia de contar hacia adelante para restar.

Contar hacia adelante es un método que sirve como ayuda para que los niños dominen la suma y la resta en operaciones hasta el 10. La meta es lograr que al final del año escolar sepan automáticamente la respuesta cuando el total sea 10 ó menos

Atentamente,
El maestro de su niño

CA CC

En la Unidad 2 se aplican los siguientes estándares auxiliares, contenidos en los *Estándares estatales comunes de matemáticas con adiciones para California*: **1.OA.1, 1.OA.3, 1.OA.5, 1.OA.6, 1.OA.7, 1.OA.8** y todos los de prácticas matemáticas.

Name

CA CC Content Standards **1.OA.5, 1.OA.6, 1.OA.8**
Mathematical Practices **MP.1, MP.6**

Count on to find the total.

1. $4 + 3 = \boxed{}$

2. $6 + 4 = \boxed{}$

3. $6 + 2 = \boxed{}$

4. $4 + 5 = \boxed{}$

5. $5 + 3 = \boxed{}$

6. $8 + 2 = \boxed{}$

7. $2 + 3 = \boxed{}$

8. $7 + 3 = \boxed{}$

9. $4 + 2 = \boxed{}$

Find the total number of toys.

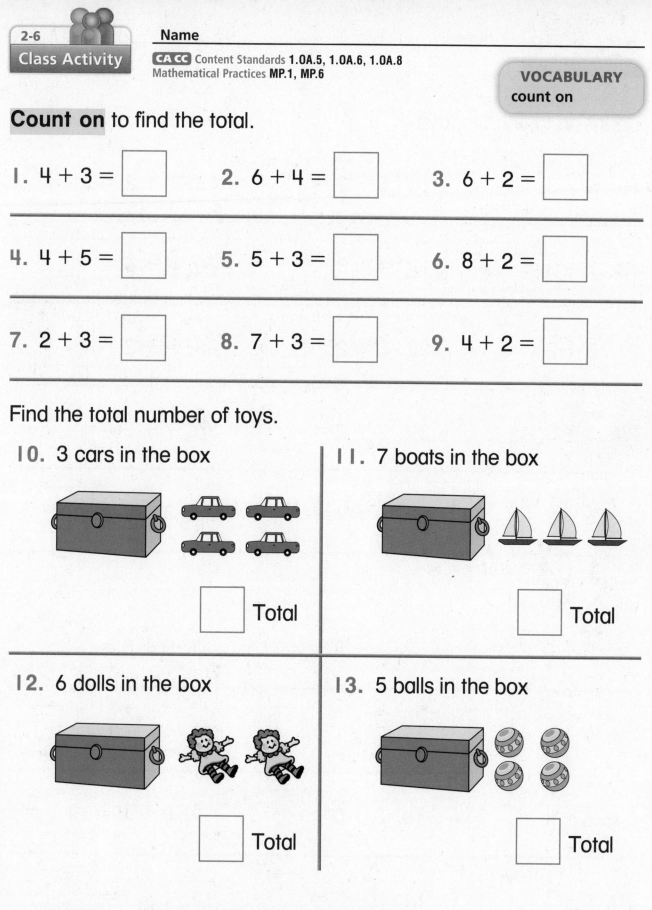

10. 3 cars in the box

$\boxed{}$ Total

11. 7 boats in the box

$\boxed{}$ Total

12. 6 dolls in the box

$\boxed{}$ Total

13. 5 balls in the box

$\boxed{}$ Total

14. Write an equation that shows a total of 10. _____

Name _____

Count on to find the total.

15. $6 + 3 =$ ☐   16. $5 + 2 =$ ☐   17. $7 + 2 =$ ☐

18. $7 + 3 =$ ☐   19. $4 + 3 =$ ☐   20. $4 + 5 =$ ☐

21. $8 + 2 =$ ☐   22. $5 + 2 =$ ☐   23. $4 + 2 =$ ☐

24. $5 + 3 =$ ☐   25. $7 + 2 =$ ☐   26. $7 + 3 =$ ☐

27. $6 + 2 =$ ☐   28. $6 + 4 =$ ☐   29. $3 + 4 =$ ☐

PATH to FLUENCY **Add.**

1. $7 + 0 =$ ☐   2. $1 + 8 =$ ☐   3. $0 + 8 =$ ☐

4. $9 + 0 =$ ☐   5. $7 + 1 =$ ☐   6. $10 + 0 =$ ☐

7. $6 + 1 =$ ☐   8. $8 + 0 =$ ☐   9. $8 + 1 =$ ☐

10. $9 + 1 =$ ☐   11. $0 + 7 =$ ☐   12. $1 + 7 =$ ☐

Addition Strategies: Counting On

Underline the greater number.
Count on from that number.

1. $3 + \underline{7} = \boxed{}$

2. $4 + 5 = \boxed{}$

3. $2 + 6 = \boxed{}$

4. $5 + 3 = \boxed{}$

5. $7 + 2 = \boxed{}$

6. $3 + 6 = \boxed{}$

7. $5 + 2 = \boxed{}$

8. $2 + 8 = \boxed{}$

9. $7 + 3 = \boxed{}$

10. $6 + 3 = \boxed{}$

11. **Tell Why** Show two ways to count on to find
the total of $6 + 3$. Which is faster?

Name _____

Underline the greater number.
Count on from that number.

12. <u>5</u> + 2 = ☐

13. 7 + 3 = ☐

14. 6 + 2 = ☐

15. 5 + 3 = ☐

16. 3 + 4 = ☐

17. 2 + 7 = ☐

18. 6 + 3 = ☐

19. 8 + 2 = ☐

20. 4 + 3 = ☐

21. 2 + 5 = ☐

22. 5 + 4 = ☐

23. 3 + 5 = ☐

24. 4 + 6 = ☐

25. 2 + 8 = ☐

26. **Explain** How did you solve Exercise 17?

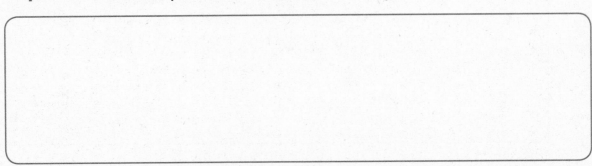

Number Quilt 1: Unknown Totals

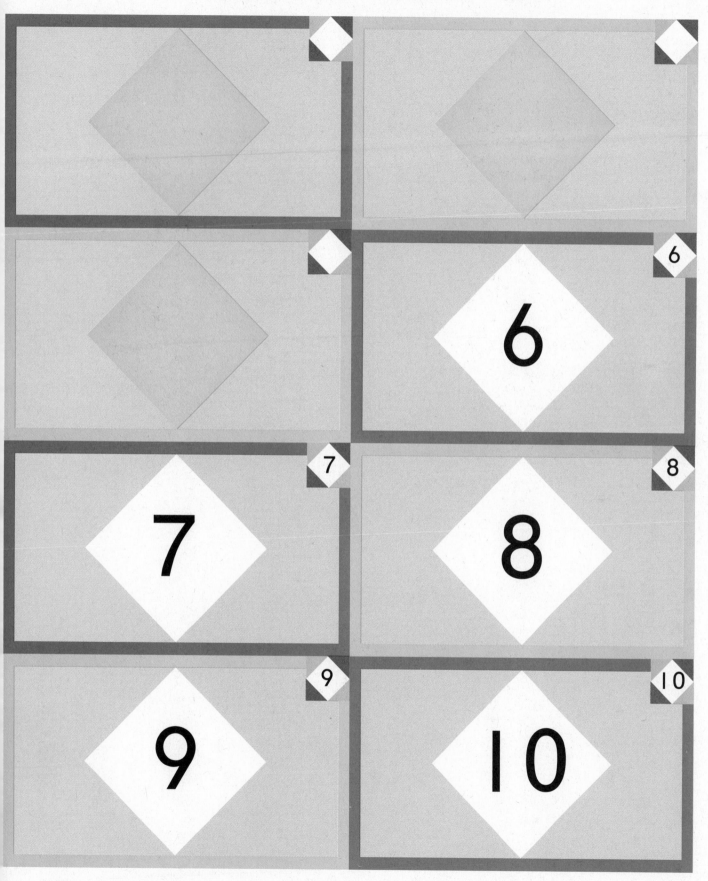

Name

CA CC Content Standards **1.OA.5, 1.OA.6, 1.OA.8**
Mathematical Practices **MP.1, MP.8**

Draw more to count on. Write how many in all.

1.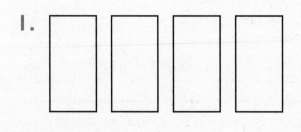

$4 + 1 =$ ☐

2.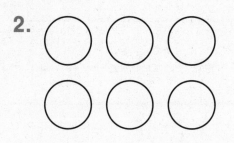

$6 + 2 =$ ☐

3.

$3 + 3 =$ ☐

4.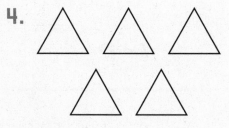

$5 + 4 =$ ☐

5.

$7 + 3 =$ ☐

Name _____

Underline the greater number.
Count on from that number.

6. $2 + \underline{8} =$ ☐   **7.** $5 + 4 =$ ☐   **8.** $6 + 3 =$ ☐

9. $7 + 3 =$ ☐   **10.** $2 + 5 =$ ☐   **11.** $3 + 4 =$ ☐

12. $4 + 3 =$ ☐   **13.** $2 + 7 =$ ☐   **14.** $8 + 2 =$ ☐

15. $3 + 6 =$ ☐   **16.** $5 + 2 =$ ☐   **17.** $6 + 2 =$ ☐

18. $5 + 3 =$ ☐   **19.** $4 + 5 =$ ☐   **20.** $2 + 6 =$ ☐

PATH to FLUENCY **Add.**

1. $3 + 2 =$ ☐   **2.** $1 + 9 =$ ☐   **3.** $7 + 0 =$ ☐

4. $8 + 1 =$ ☐   **5.** $0 + 9 =$ ☐   **6.** $1 + 6 =$ ☐

7. $8 + 0 =$ ☐   **8.** $7 + 1 =$ ☐   **9.** $2 + 3 =$ ☐

10. $0 + 10 =$ ☐   **11.** $9 + 0 =$ ☐   **12.** $9 + 1 =$ ☐

Addition Games: Unknown Totals

Name Shea

CA CC Content Standards **1.0A.6, 1.0A.7**
Mathematical Practices **MP.2**

VOCABULARY
subtract

Subtract and write the equation.

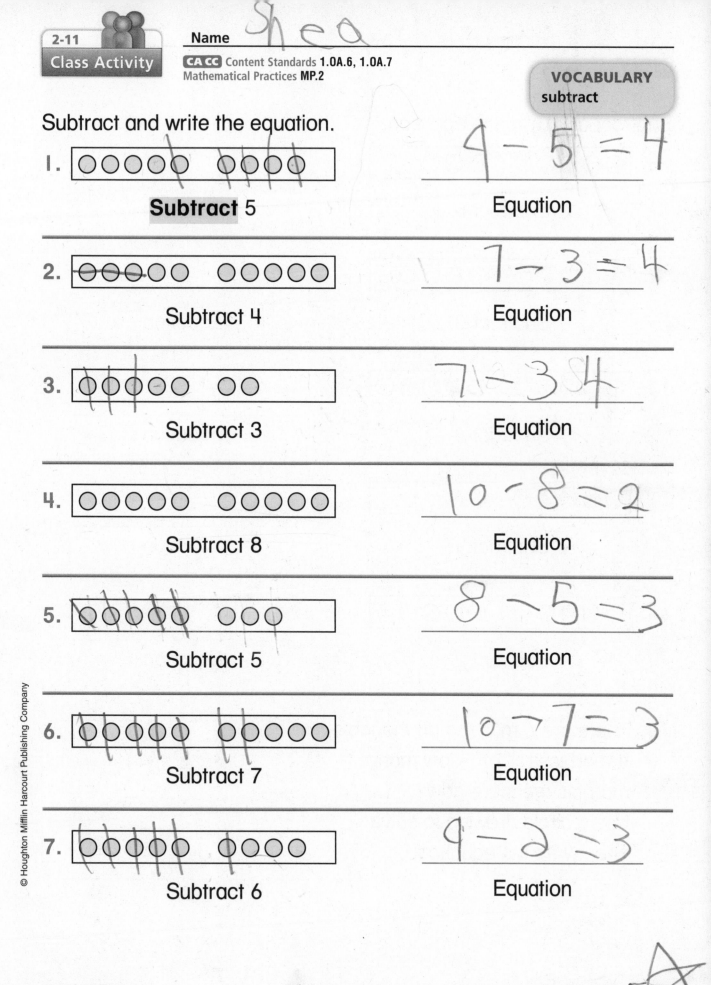

1. $9 - 5 = 4$

Subtract 5 — Equation

2. $7 - 3 = 4$

Subtract 4 — Equation

3. $7 - 3 \ 4$

Subtract 3 — Equation

4. $10 - 8 = 2$

Subtract 8 — Equation

5. $8 - 5 = 3$

Subtract 5 — Equation

6. $10 - 7 = 3$

Subtract 7 — Equation

7. $9 - 2 = 3$

Subtract 6 — Equation

Name _____

Subtract and write the equation.

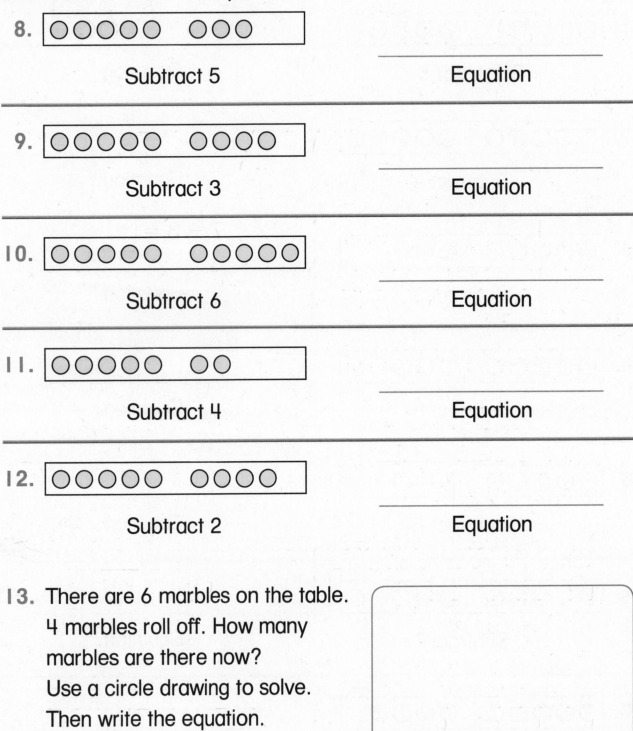

8. ○○○○○ ○○○

Subtract 5   _____
                                 Equation

9. ○○○○○ ○○○○

Subtract 3   _____
                                 Equation

10. ○○○○○ ○○○○○

Subtract 6   _____
                                 Equation

11. ○○○○○ ○○

Subtract 4   _____
                                 Equation

12. ○○○○○ ○○○○

Subtract 2   _____
                                 Equation

13. There are 6 marbles on the table.
4 marbles roll off. How many
marbles are there now?
Use a circle drawing to solve.
Then write the equation.

Subtraction with Drawings and Equations

Name

CA CC Content Standards **1.0A.6, 1.0A.8**
Mathematical Practices **MP.2**

Use the picture to solve the equation.

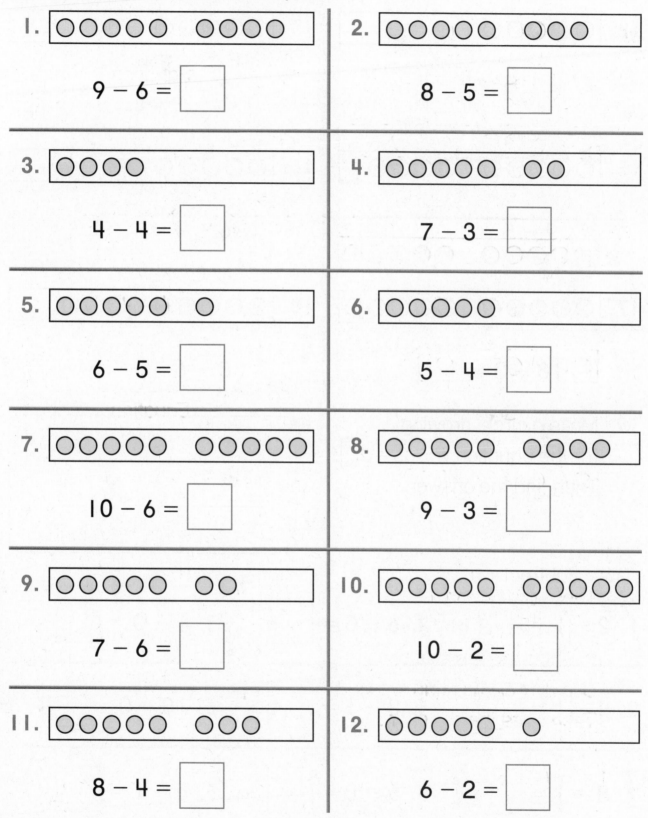

1. $9 - 6 = \boxed{}$

2. $8 - 5 = \boxed{}$

3. $4 - 4 = \boxed{}$

4. $7 - 3 = \boxed{}$

5. $6 - 5 = \boxed{}$

6. $5 - 4 = \boxed{}$

7. $10 - 6 = \boxed{}$

8. $9 - 3 = \boxed{}$

9. $7 - 6 = \boxed{}$

10. $10 - 2 = \boxed{}$

11. $8 - 4 = \boxed{}$

12. $6 - 2 = \boxed{}$

Use the picture to solve the equation.

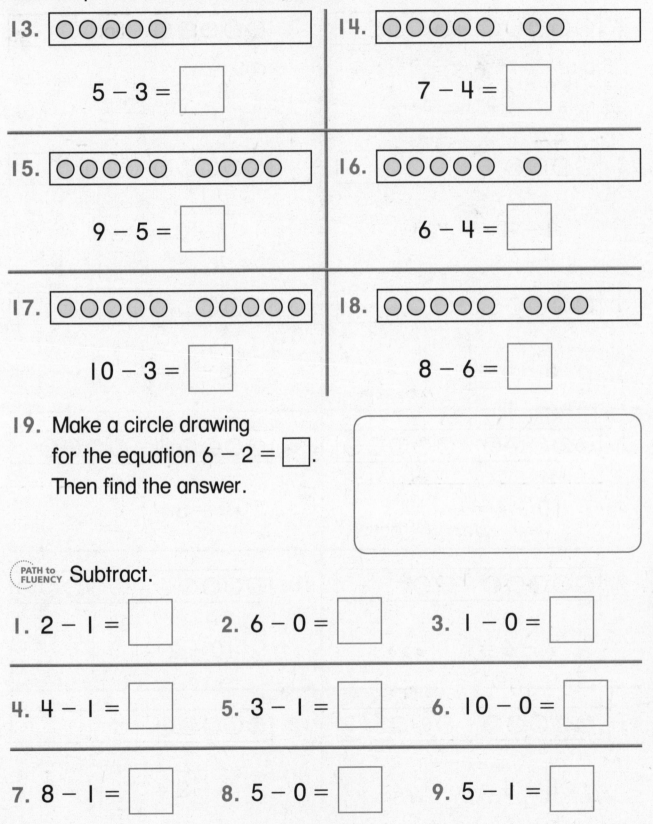

13. ⊙⊙⊙⊙⊙

$5 - 3 = \boxed{}$

14. ⊙⊙⊙⊙⊙ ⊙⊙

$7 - 4 = \boxed{}$

15. ⊙⊙⊙⊙⊙ ⊙⊙⊙⊙

$9 - 5 = \boxed{}$

16. ⊙⊙⊙⊙⊙ ○

$6 - 4 = \boxed{}$

17. ⊙⊙⊙⊙⊙ ⊙⊙⊙⊙⊙

$10 - 3 = \boxed{}$

18. ⊙⊙⊙⊙⊙ ○○○

$8 - 6 = \boxed{}$

19. Make a circle drawing
for the equation $6 - 2 = \boxed{}$.
Then find the answer.

PATH to FLUENCY Subtract.

1. $2 - 1 = \boxed{}$ 2. $6 - 0 = \boxed{}$ 3. $1 - 0 = \boxed{}$

4. $4 - 1 = \boxed{}$ 5. $3 - 1 = \boxed{}$ 6. $10 - 0 = \boxed{}$

7. $8 - 1 = \boxed{}$ 8. $5 - 0 = \boxed{}$ 9. $5 - 1 = \boxed{}$

Practice with Subtraction

Name

CA CC Content Standards **1.0A.1, 1.0A.6**
Mathematical Practices **MP.1, MP.6, MP.7, MP.8**

Relate addition and subtraction.

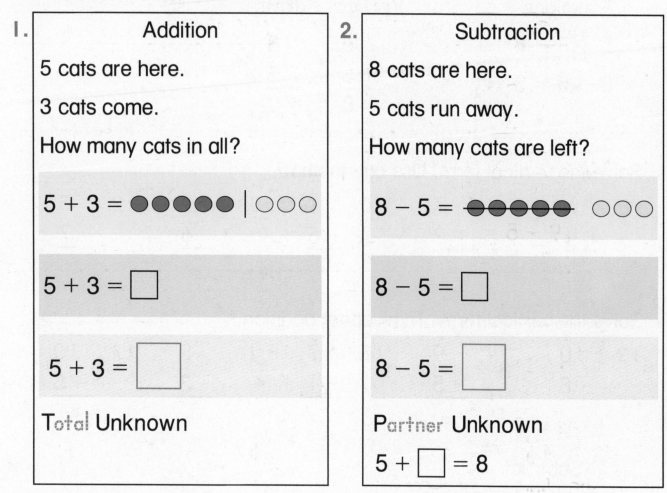

1. Addition

5 cats are here.

3 cats come.

How many cats in all?

$5 + 3 =$ ●●●●● | ○○○

$5 + 3 = \square$

$5 + 3 = \square$

Total Unknown

2. Subtraction

8 cats are here.

5 cats run away.

How many cats are left?

$8 - 5 =$ ●●●●● ○○○

$8 - 5 = \square$

$8 - 5 = \square$

Partner Unknown

$5 + \square = 8$

Use addition to solve subtraction.

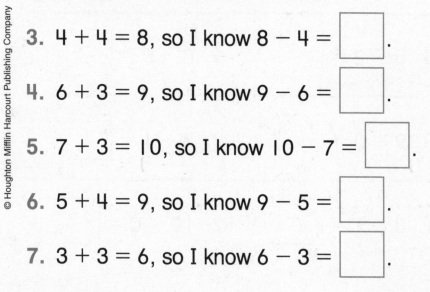

3. $4 + 4 = 8$, so I know $8 - 4 = \square$.

4. $6 + 3 = 9$, so I know $9 - 6 = \square$.

5. $7 + 3 = 10$, so I know $10 - 7 = \square$.

6. $5 + 4 = 9$, so I know $9 - 5 = \square$.

7. $3 + 3 = 6$, so I know $6 - 3 = \square$.

VOCABULARY
vertical forms

Equations	**Vertical Forms**	
$5 + 3 = 8$	5	8
$8 - 5 = 3$	$+\ 3$	$-\ 5$
	8	3

Solve the vertical form. Use any method.

8.	9.	10.	11.	12.
6	7	1	2	3
$+\ 4$	$+\ 2$	$+\ 6$	$+\ 6$	$+\ 7$

Solve the vertical form. Think about addition.

13.	14.	15.	16.	17.
10	9	7	8	10
$-\ 8$	$-\ 5$	$-\ 1$	$-\ 3$	$-\ 5$

PATH to FLUENCY Subtract.

1. $4 - 0 =$ ☐   2. $6 - 1 =$ ☐   3. $4 - 2 =$ ☐

4. $9 - 1 =$ ☐   5. $5 - 2 =$ ☐   6. $8 - 0 =$ ☐

7. $3 - 2 =$ ☐   8. $9 - 0 =$ ☐   9. $7 - 1 =$ ☐

10. $6 - 0 =$ ☐   11. $8 - 1 =$ ☐   12. $10 - 0 =$ ☐

Relate Addition and Subtraction

CA CC Content Standards **1.OA.1, 1.OA.6, 1.OA.8**
Mathematical Practices **MP.1, MP.4, MP.5**

▶ Math and the Animal Park

Darya and her family go to the animal park.

Use the picture to solve the equation.

1. Darya sees 5 lions. Then she sees 3 more lions.

How many lions does she see in all? $5 + 3 =$ ☐

2. Nick sees 9 crocodiles in the water.

Then 2 crocodiles climb out.

How many crocodiles are in the water now? $9 - 2 =$ ☐

Name _____

Use the picture to solve the equation.

3. Ray sees 1 cheetah in a tree and 7 lions under a tree.

How many wild cats does he see?   1 + 7 = ☐

---

4. Sophie sees 8 baboons and 2 mandrills.

How many monkeys does she see?   8 + 2 = ☐

Focus on Mathematical Practices

Write the partners and the total.

1.

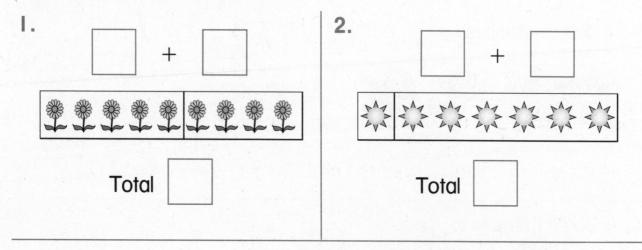

☐ + ☐

Total ☐

2.

☐ + ☐

Total ☐

3. Does the equation match the circle drawing?
Choose Yes or No.

$3 + 2 = 5$

○ Yes   ○ No

$5 + 2 = 7$

○ Yes   ○ No

$6 + 3 = 9$

○ Yes   ○ No

Ring the total number of toys in the group.

4. 7 dolls in the box

7
9
0

Total

5. 4 boats in the box

7
9
1

Total

6. Ring a number to show the cars
   in the box. Write the total.

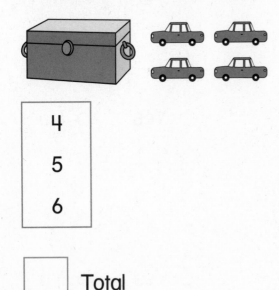

4
5
6

Total

7. Solve. Match the story or circle drawing to the equation.

There are 8 apples.

 •

Then 3 are eaten.

• $9 - 3 = 6$

There are 7 flowers.

 •

Then 5 are picked.

• $10 - 6 = 4$

Subtract 3

 •

• $7 - 5 = 2$

Subtract 6

 •

• $8 - 3 = 5$

8. Make a circle drawing

for the equation $6 - 4 = \boxed{}$.

Then find the answer.

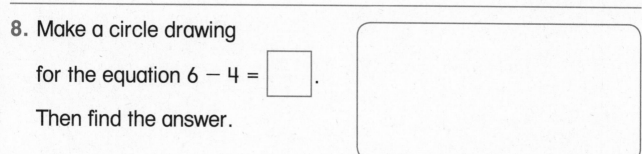

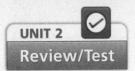
9. Write the subtraction equation below the
   addition equation that helps you solve it.

| $10 - 2 = 8$ | $8 - 5 = 3$ | $9 - 4 = 5$ |

$3 + 5 = 8$ $5 + 4 = 9$ $8 + 2 = 10$

_____   _____   _____

10. Write an equation for the story. Make a
    Proof Drawing to show that the equation is
    true. Write the vertical form.

> There are 7 flowers in the vase.
>
> Lily puts 2 more flowers in the vase.
>
> Now there are 9 flowers.

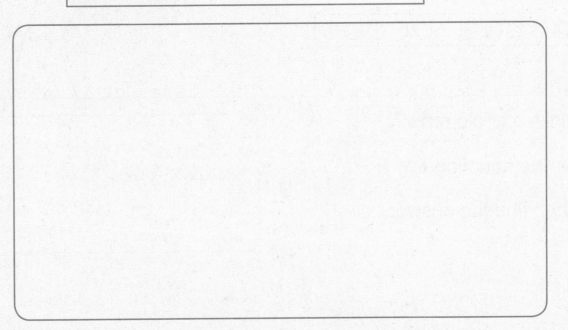

Dear Family:

Your child has started a new unit on story problems. Because most children this age are learning to read, your child may need help reading the story problems. Offer help when it is needed, but do not give the answer.

To solve story problems, children first need to know which number is unknown. Is it the total or one of the parts? This program helps children focus on this important issue by using "Math Mountains." In a Math Mountain, the total sits at the top and the parts (or partners) sit at the bottom of the mountain. Children can quickly see the relationship between the partners and the total when they look at the mountain.

Math Mountain

Math Mountains are especially helpful in showing children how to find an unknown partner, as in the following problem: *I see 9 horses. 5 are black, and the others are white. How many horses are white?*

Children can find the answer by drawing the mountain to see which number is unknown. Then they count on from the partner they know to the total. In this way, they can find the partner they don't know.

Math Mountain with Unknown Partner

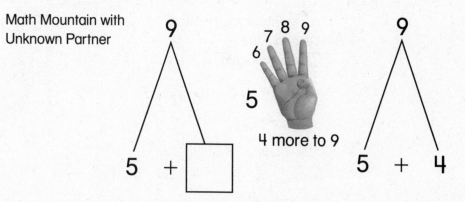

4 more to 9

If you have any questions, please contact me.

Sincerely,
Your child's teacher

© Houghton Mifflin Harcourt Publishing Company

 CA CC

Unit 3 addresses the following standards from the *Common Core State Standards for Mathematics with California Additions*: **1.OA.1, 1.OA.4, 1.OA.5, 1.OA.6, 1.OA.8,** and all Mathematical Practices.

Carta a la familia

Un vistazo general al contenido

Estimada familia:

Su niño ha empezado una nueva unidad donde aprenderá cómo resolver problemas matemáticos. Como la mayoría de los niños a esta edad aún están aprendiendo a leer, es probable que su niño necesite ayuda para leer los problemas. Ofrezca ayuda cuando haga falta, pero no dé la respuesta.

Para resolver problemas, los niños primero deben hallar el número desconocido. ¿Es el total o una de las partes? Este programa los ayuda a concentrarse en este punto importante usando "Montañas matemáticas". En una montaña matemática el total está en la cima y las partes están al pie de la montaña. Al ver la montaña, los niños pueden ver rápidamente la relación entre las partes y el total.

6

4 + 2

Montaña matemática

Las montañas matemáticas son especialmente útiles para mostrar a los niños cómo hallar una parte desconocida, como en el problema siguiente: *Veo 9 caballos. 5 son negros y los demás son blancos. ¿Cuántos caballos son blancos?*

Los niños pueden hallar la respuesta dibujando la montaña para saber cuál es el número desconocido. Luego, cuentan hacia adelante a partir de la parte que conocen para hallar el total. De esta manera, pueden hallar la parte desconocida.

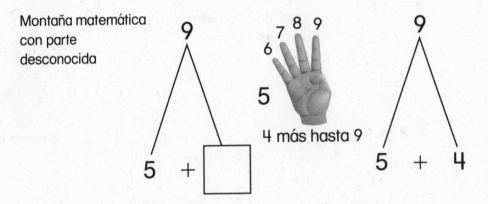

Montaña matemática con parte desconocida

9

5 + ☐

6 7 8 9

5

4 más hasta 9

9

5 + 4

Si tiene alguna pregunta, por favor comuníquese conmigo.

Atentamente,
El maestro de su niño

© Houghton Mifflin Harcourt Publishing Company

CA CC

En la Unidad 3 se aplican los siguientes estándares auxiliares, contenidos en los *Estándares estatales comunes de matemáticas con adiciones para California*: **1.0A.1, 1.0A.4, 1.0A.5, 1.0A.6, 1.0A.8** y todos los de prácticas matemáticas.

Explore Unknowns

Name

CA CC Content Standards **1.0A.5, 1.0A.6**
Mathematical Practices **MP.5, MP.6**

Find the **unknown partner**.

1.
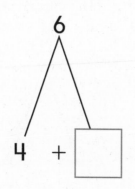
6

4 + ☐

2.
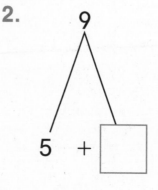
9

5 + ☐

3.
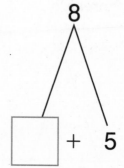
8

☐ + 5

4.
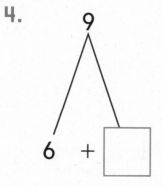
9

6 + ☐

5.
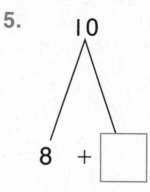
10

8 + ☐

6.
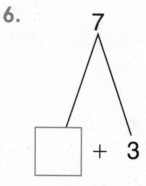
7

☐ + 3

7.
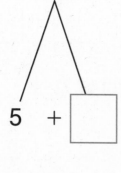
10

5 + ☐

8.
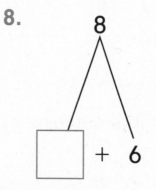
8

☐ + 6

9.
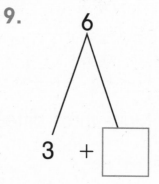
6

3 + ☐

10.
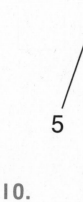
9

4 + ☐

11.
5

☐ + 2

12.
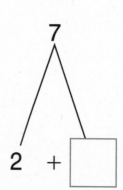
7

2 + ☐

Name _____

13. Make three different Math Mountains with a total of 10.

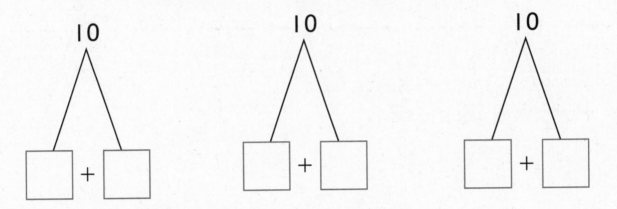

14. Make three different Math Mountains with a total of 8.

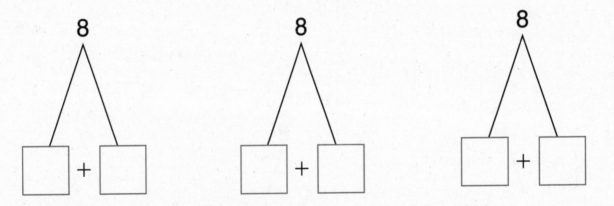

15. Make three different Math Mountains with a total of 7.

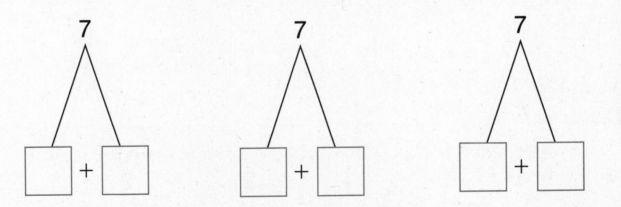

Explore Unknowns

Name _____

CA CC Content Standards **1.OA.1**
Mathematical Practices **MP.1, MP.4, MP.5**

VOCABULARY
story problem
label

Solve the **story problem**.

Show your work. Use drawings, numbers, or words.

---

1. We see 9 fish.

   5 are big. The others are small.

   How many fish are small?

   ☐ _____
   label

fish

---

2. 8 boys are riding bikes.

   6 ride fast. The rest ride slow.

   How many boys ride slow?

   ☐ _____
   label

bike

---

3. Ana has 2 hats.

   Then she gets more.

   Now she has 5.

   How many hats does she get?

   ☐ _____
   label

hat

---

4. Discuss why it is important to write a **label** in the answer.

Solve the story problem. Use cubes to help.

5. Raja has 6 plums. He wants to put some on each of two plates. How many can he put on each plate? Show 4 answers.

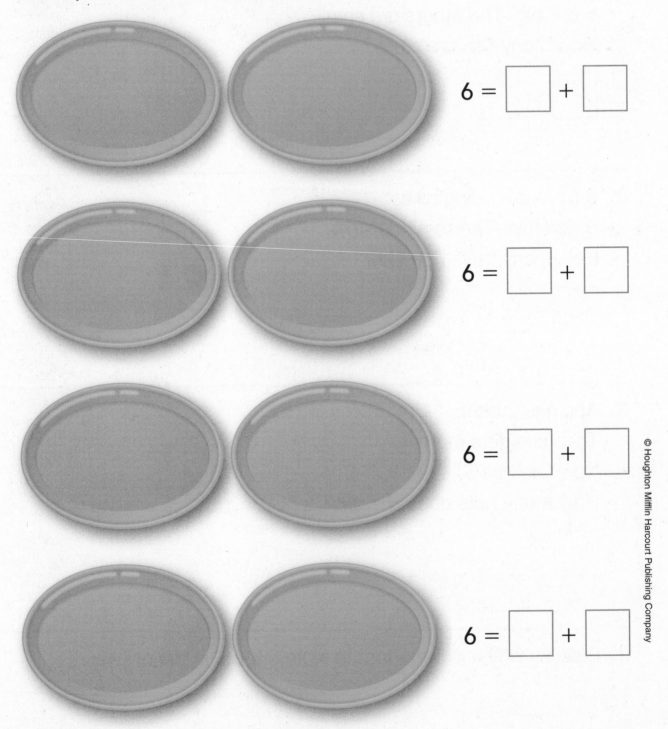

$6 = \boxed{} + \boxed{}$

$6 = \boxed{} + \boxed{}$

$6 = \boxed{} + \boxed{}$

$6 = \boxed{} + \boxed{}$

Problems with Unknown Partners

Count on to find the unknown partner.

1. $3 + \boxed{} = 6$ 2. $7 + \boxed{} = 10$ 3. $2 + \boxed{} = 6$

4. $7 + \boxed{} = 9$ 5. $4 + \boxed{} = 8$ 6. $5 + \boxed{} = 8$

Count on to solve.

7. 6 letters total

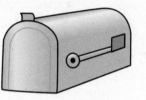

How many letters
are in the box? $\boxed{}$ _____
                              label

8. 10 footprints total

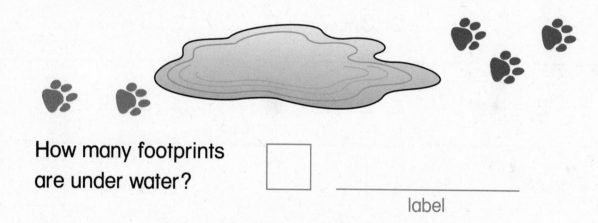

How many footprints
are under water? $\boxed{}$ _____
                               label

9. Look at Puzzled Penguin's work.

$2 + \boxed{} = 8$

$2 + \boxed{10} = 8$

Am I correct?

10. Help Puzzled Penguin.

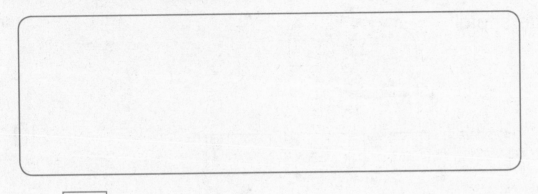

$2 + \boxed{} = 8$

PATH to FLUENCY **Add.**

1. $4 + 4 = \boxed{}$ 2. $3 + 7 = \boxed{}$ 3. $3 + 3 = \boxed{}$

4. $8 + 2 = \boxed{}$ 5. $2 + 2 = \boxed{}$ 6. $6 + 4 = \boxed{}$

7. $1 + 1 = \boxed{}$ 8. $1 + 9 = \boxed{}$ 9. $5 + 5 = \boxed{}$

10. $7 + 3 = \boxed{}$ 11. $2 + 8 = \boxed{}$ 12. $4 + 6 = \boxed{}$

Solve Equations with Unknown Partners

$3 + \boxed{} = 6$ $\qquad$ $3 + \boxed{} = 7$ $\qquad$ $3 + \boxed{} = 8$

$3 + \boxed{} = 9$ $\qquad$ $3 + \boxed{} = 10$ $\qquad$ $4 + \boxed{} = 7$

$4 + \boxed{} = 8$ $\qquad$ $4 + \boxed{} = 9$ $\qquad$ $4 + \boxed{} = 10$

$5 + \boxed{} = 8$ $\qquad$ $5 + \boxed{} = 9$ $\qquad$ $5 + \boxed{} = 10$

$6 + \boxed{} = 9$ $\qquad$ $6 + \boxed{} = 10$ $\qquad$ $7 + \boxed{} = 10$

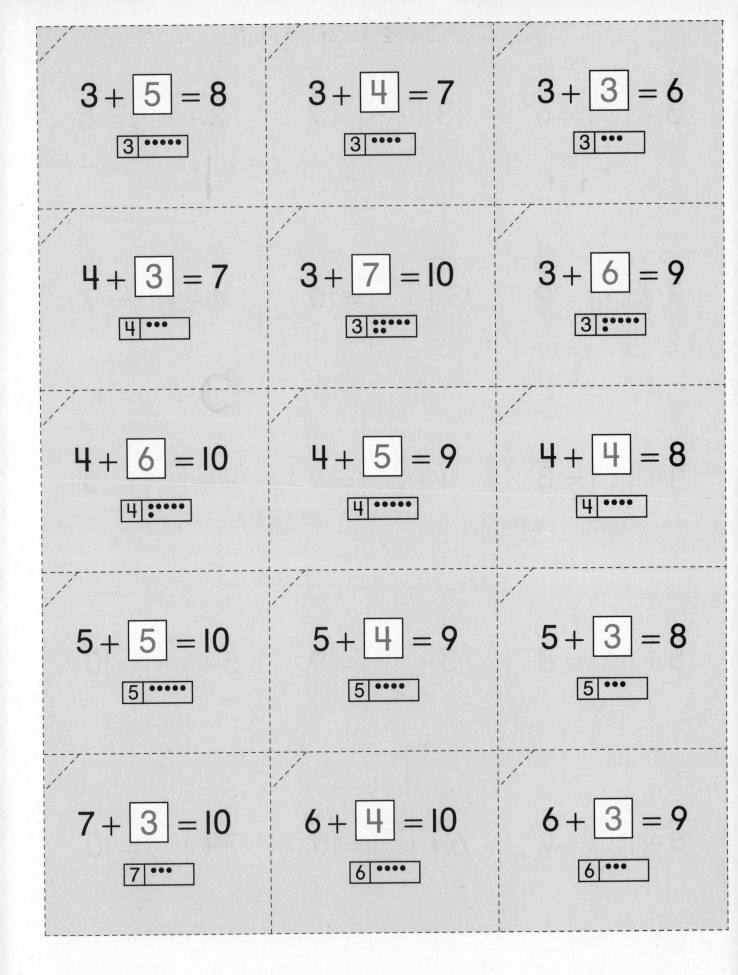

$3 + \boxed{5} = 8$

$3 + \boxed{4} = 7$

$3 + \boxed{3} = 6$

$4 + \boxed{3} = 7$

$3 + \boxed{7} = 10$

$3 + \boxed{6} = 9$

$4 + \boxed{6} = 10$

$4 + \boxed{5} = 9$

$4 + \boxed{4} = 8$

$5 + \boxed{5} = 10$

$5 + \boxed{4} = 9$

$5 + \boxed{3} = 8$

$7 + \boxed{3} = 10$

$6 + \boxed{4} = 10$

$6 + \boxed{3} = 9$

Yellow Count-On Cards

Number Quilt 2: Unknown Partners

UNIT 3 LESSON 4
© Houghton Mifflin Harcourt Publishing Company

Number Quilt 2 **75**
Use with the Yellow or Orange Count-On Cards.

Name _____

CA CC Content Standards **1.0A.1**
Mathematical Practices **MP.1, MP.6**

Solve the story problem.

Show your work. Use drawings, numbers, or words.

1. Sam has 4 balloons.

   Then he gets some more.

   Now he has 9.

   How many balloons does he get?

   ☐ _____
   label

balloon

2. There are 8 crayons on the table.

   5 are red.

   The others are green.

   How many crayons are green?

   ☐ _____
   label

table

3. Rabia sees 10 eagles.

   3 are in a tree.

   The rest are flying.

   How many eagles are flying?

   ☐ _____
   label

eagle

Addition Game: Unknown Partners **77**

Name _____

Solve the story problem.

Show your work. Use drawings, numbers, or words.

---

4. Maddox has 3 toy trains.
   Then he gets more.
   Now he has 7.
   How many trains does he get?

   [ ] _____
         label

train

---

5. We pick 10 apples from the trees.
   6 are green. Some are red.
   How many apples are red?

   [ ] _____
         label

tree

---

6. Milena wants to put 8 balls
   in a box. She wants to have
   soccer balls and footballs.
   How many of each ball could
   she use? Show three answers.

soccer ball

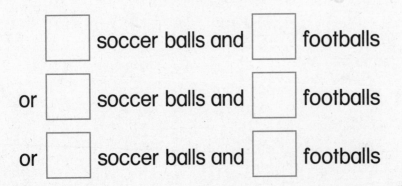

   [ ] soccer balls and [ ] footballs

   or [ ] soccer balls and [ ] footballs

   or [ ] soccer balls and [ ] footballs

Addition Game: Unknown Partners

Name

CA CC Content Standards **1.OA.1, 1.OA.6, 1.OA.8**
Mathematical Practices **MP.1, MP.4**

VOCABULARY
subtraction story problem

Solve the **subtraction story problem**. Show your work. Use drawings, numbers, or words.

---

1. 8 flies are on a log.
6 are eaten by a frog.
How many flies are left?

[2] flies
_____
label

frog

---

2. I find 7 shells by the sea.
Then I lose 3 of them.
How many shells do I
have now?

[4] shells
_____
label

shell

---

3. I draw 10 houses.
Then I erase 5 of them.
How many houses are left?

[5] houses
_____
label

house

---

4. Write a subtraction story problem.

I have 9 kioves
4 cookes with my
friends. I

5. Write an equation to solve.

Use a box for the unknown number.

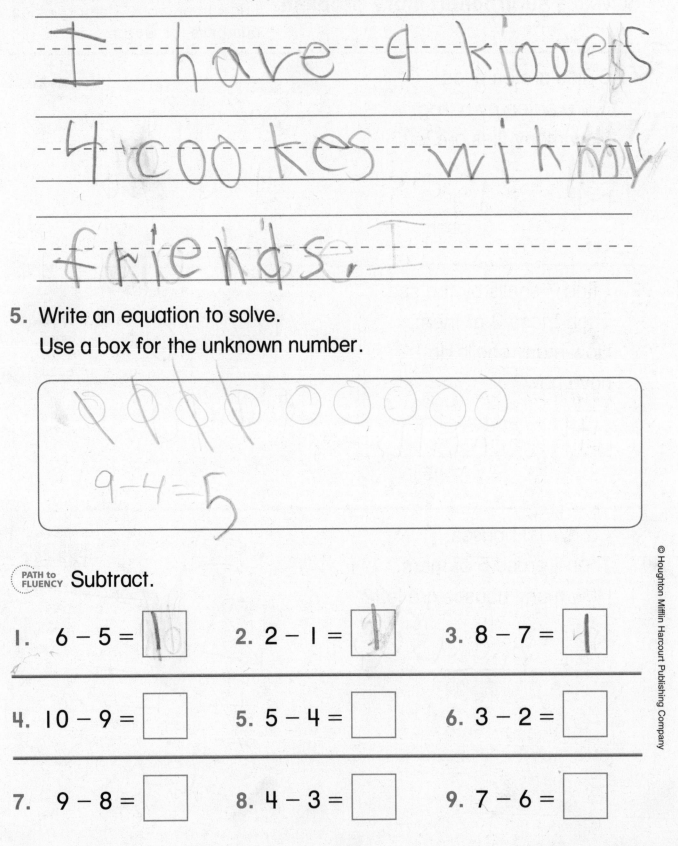

9 − 4 = 5

PATH to FLUENCY Subtract.

1. 6 − 5 = [1]   **2.** 2 − 1 = [1]   **3.** 8 − 7 = [1]

4. 10 − 9 = [ ]   **5.** 5 − 4 = [ ]   **6.** 3 − 2 = [ ]

7. 9 − 8 = [ ]   **8.** 4 − 3 = [ ]   **9.** 7 − 6 = [ ]

6 − 3 = ☐   7 − 3 = ☐   8 − 3 = ☐

9 − 3 = ☐   10 − 3 = ☐   7 − 4 = ☐

8 − 4 = ☐   9 − 4 = ☐   10 − 4 = ☐

8 − 5 = ☐   9 − 5 = ☐   10 − 5 = ☐

9 − 6 = ☐   10 − 6 = ☐   10 − 7 = ☐

$8 - 3 = \boxed{5}$

$\boxed{3}\ |\ \boxed{\bullet\bullet\bullet\bullet\bullet}$

$7 - 3 = \boxed{4}$

$\boxed{3}\ |\ \boxed{\bullet\bullet\bullet\bullet}$

$6 - 3 = \boxed{3}$

$\boxed{3}\ |\ \boxed{\bullet\bullet\bullet}$

$7 - 4 = \boxed{3}$

$\boxed{4}\ |\ \boxed{\bullet\bullet\bullet}$

$10 - 3 = \boxed{7}$

$\boxed{3}\ |\ \boxed{\bullet\bullet\bullet\bullet\bullet}$

$9 - 3 = \boxed{6}$

$\boxed{3}\ |\ \boxed{\bullet\bullet\bullet\bullet\bullet}$

$10 - 4 = \boxed{6}$

$\boxed{4}\ |\ \boxed{\bullet\bullet\bullet\bullet}$

$9 - 4 = \boxed{5}$

$\boxed{4}\ |\ \boxed{\bullet\bullet\bullet\bullet\bullet}$

$8 - 4 = \boxed{4}$

$\boxed{4}\ |\ \boxed{\bullet\bullet\bullet\bullet}$

$10 - 5 = \boxed{5}$

$\boxed{5}\ |\ \boxed{\bullet\bullet\bullet\bullet\bullet}$

$9 - 5 = \boxed{4}$

$\boxed{5}\ |\ \boxed{\bullet\bullet\bullet\bullet}$

$8 - 5 = \boxed{3}$

$\boxed{5}\ |\ \boxed{\bullet\bullet\bullet}$

$10 - 7 = \boxed{3}$

$\boxed{7}\ |\ \boxed{\bullet\bullet\bullet}$

$10 - 6 = \boxed{4}$

$\boxed{6}\ |\ \boxed{\bullet\bullet\bullet\bullet}$

$9 - 6 = \boxed{3}$

$\boxed{6}\ |\ \boxed{\bullet\bullet\bullet}$

Orange Count-On Cards

Solve and discuss.

1. We see 10 dogs.
   7 run away.
   How many are left?

   ⬜ _____
         label

2. We see 9 dogs.
   5 are not barking.
   The rest are barking.
   How many are barking?

   ⬜ _____
         label

3. **Discuss** How are the methods you used to solve the problems alike and different?

Name _____

Solve the story problem.

Show your work. Use drawings, numbers, or words.

4. There are 8 apples. 6 apples are eaten.
   How many apples are there now?

   ☐ _____

   label

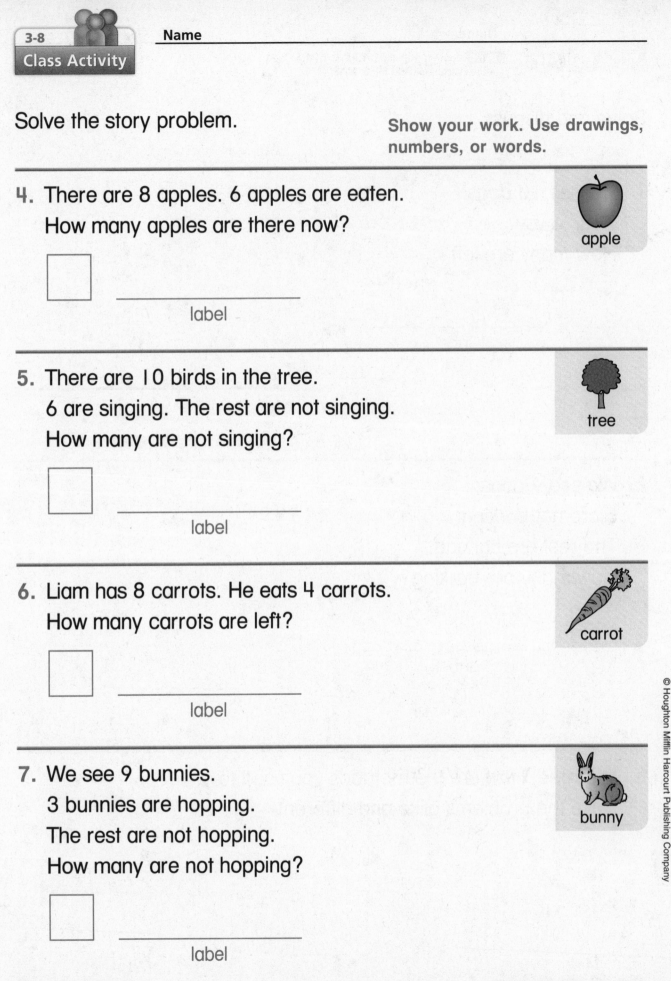

apple

5. There are 10 birds in the tree.
   6 are singing. The rest are not singing.
   How many are not singing?

   ☐ _____

   label

tree

6. Liam has 8 carrots. He eats 4 carrots.
   How many carrots are left?

   ☐ _____

   label

carrot

7. We see 9 bunnies.
   3 bunnies are hopping.
   The rest are not hopping.
   How many are not hopping?

   ☐ _____

   label

bunny

Practice with Subtraction Stories

Solve and discuss.

1. There are 4 cats.
3 more cats join them.
How many cats are there now?

$4 + 3 = \boxed{}$

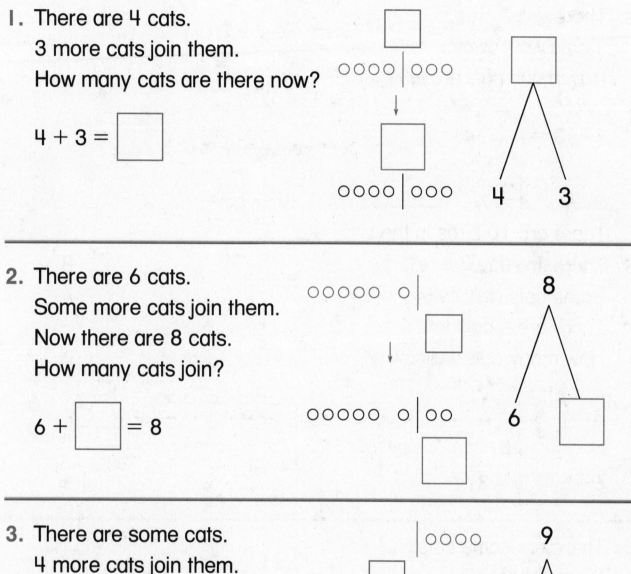

2. There are 6 cats.
Some more cats join them.
Now there are 8 cats.
How many cats join?

$6 + \boxed{} = 8$

3. There are some cats.
4 more cats join them.
Now there are 9 cats.
How many cats are there
at the start?

$\boxed{} + 4 = 9$

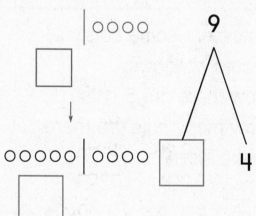

Name _____

Solve and discuss.

4. There are 7 cats.
3 cats walk away.
How many cats are left?

$7 - 3 = \boxed{}$

$3 + \boxed{} = 7$

7

3

---

5. There are 8 cats.
Some cats walk away.
There are 6 cats left.
How many cats walk away?

$8 - \boxed{} = 6$

$6 + \boxed{} = 8$

8

6

---

6. There are some cats.
4 cats walk away.
Now there are 5 cats.
How many cats are there
at the start?

$\boxed{} - 4 = 5$

$5 + 4 = \boxed{}$

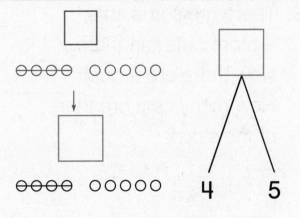

4   5

Relate Addition and Subtraction Situations

Solve the story problem.

7. 10 kittens are in the bed. 7 are not sleeping. The rest are sleeping. How many are sleeping?

kitten

_____
label

8. Emma has 5 beads. She gets some more beads. Now she has 9 beads. How many beads does she get?

bead

_____
label

9. 8 boys are at the park. Some boys go home. 3 boys are left. How many boys go home?

boy

_____
label

10. Some horses are in the barn. 3 more horses go in. 7 horses are in the barn now. How many are there at the start?

barn

_____
label

Solve the story problem.

11. Dad picks some flowers. He puts 2 in the red vase and the other 5 in the blue vase. How many does he pick?

flower

☐ _____
label

12. There are some tomatoes. Bugs eat 6. There are 4 left. How many tomatoes are there at first?

tomato

☐ _____
label

13. There are 5 puppies. Then 3 more puppies come. How many puppies are there now?

puppy

☐ _____
label

14. 9 people go for a bike ride. 6 go up hill. The others go by the pond. How many go by the pond?

pond

☐ _____
label

Relate Addition and Subtraction Situations

Name _____

CA CC Content Standards **1.0A.1, 1.0A.4, 1.0A.6**
Mathematical Practices **MP.1, MP.4**

Solve.

1. Sam scores 4 points. Julio scores 3 points. How many points do they score in all?

2. Sam scores 4 points. Julio also scores some points. In all they score 7 points. How many points does Julio score?

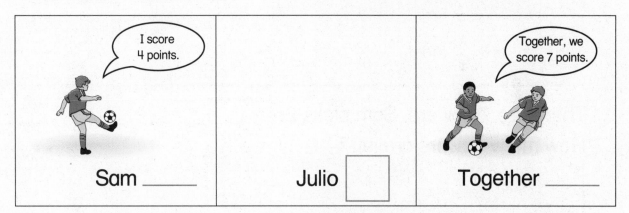

3. Sam scores some points. Then Julio scores 3 points. In all they score 7 points. How many points does Sam score?

Solve the story problem.

Show your work. Use drawings, numbers, or words.

4. 8 frogs are in the pond. Some hop away.
   2 are left. How many frogs hop away?

   ☐ _____
       label

   pond

5. Ivan has some balls.
   He gives 4 to friends.
   He has 3 left. How many
   did he have before?

   ☐ _____
       label

   ball

6. There are 7 flowers. Sam picks 2.
   How many flowers are left?

   ☐ _____
       label

   flower

PATH to FLUENCY **Subtract.**

1. $2 - 2 =$ ☐

2. $4 - 2 =$ ☐

3. $4 - 4 =$ ☐

4. $8 - 4 =$ ☐

5. $5 - 5 =$ ☐

6. $10 - 5 =$ ☐

Solve Mixed Problems

Number Quilt 3: Any Unknown

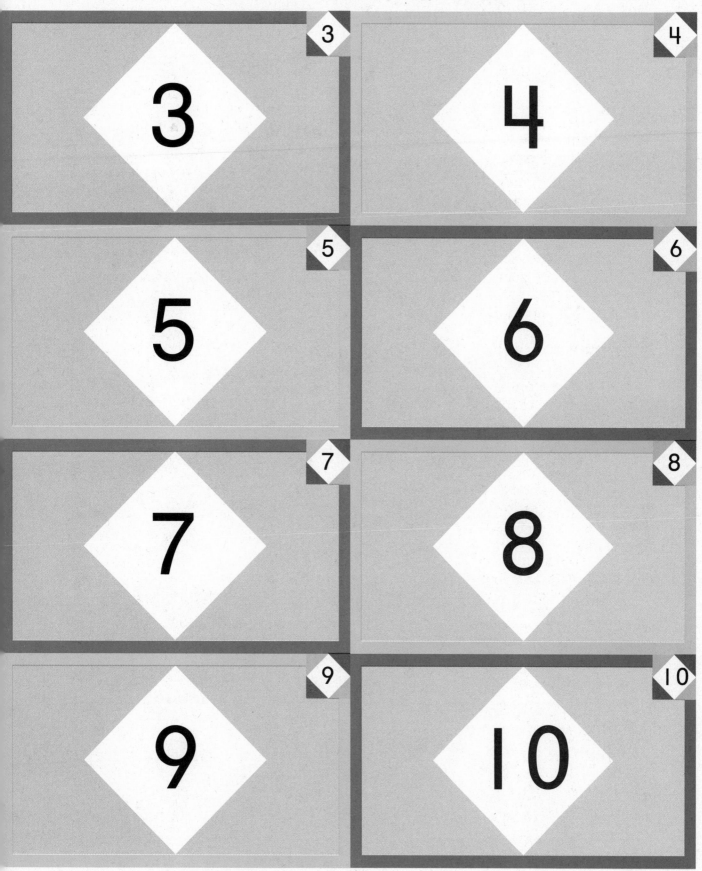

Name _____

CA CC Content Standards **1.0A.1**
Mathematical Practices **MP.1, MP.2, MP.4, MP.5**

Math and Sports

Write the equation to solve.

1. There are 7 balls in the box. Jabar puts some more balls in the box. Now there are 10 balls in the box. How many balls does Jabar put in the box?

☐ ○ ☐ = ☐

☐ balls

2. There were 8 baseballs in the bucket. Leslie takes some baseballs from the bucket. Now there are 6 baseballs in the bucket. How many baseballs does Leslie take?

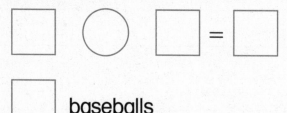

☐ ○ ☐ = ☐

☐ baseballs

3. Use the picture to write a story problem.
Write and solve the equation.

_____

- -

_____

_____

- -

_____

_____

- -

_____

□ ◯ □ = □

□ _____

label

Focus on Mathematical Practices

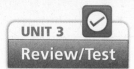
1. Match each set of partners to a total.

$6 + 2 =$ _____ •   • 5

$9 - 3 =$ _____ •   • 10

$3 + 7 =$ _____ •   • 8

$8 - 3 =$ _____ •   • 6

Make three different Math Mountains with a total of 6.

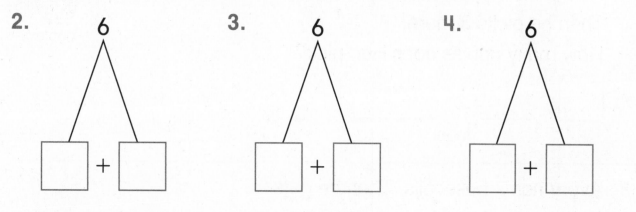

2.   3.   4.

5. Count on to solve.

8 rakes total

How many rakes are in the shed?

[ ] _____
        label

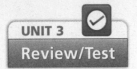
Name _____

Solve the story problem.

6. Maisy has 5 balloons. She gets some
   more balloons. Now she has 9 balloons.
   How many balloons does Maisy get?

   balloon

   [ ] _____
        label

7. Han picks 5 apples.
   Then he picks 3 more.
   How many apples does Han pick?

   apple

   [ ] _____
        label

8. Avery has 7 baseballs. Then he gets
   some more. Now Avery has 10 baseballs.
   How many baseballs does he get?

   ball

   [ ] _____
        label

Complete the number sentences.
Use the numbers on the tiles.

| 6 | 5 | 4 | 8 |

9. $10 - \boxed{} = 2$

10. $4 + \boxed{} = 8$

11. $3 + \boxed{} = 9$

12. $8 - \boxed{} = 3$

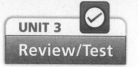
Ring the number that
makes the sentence true.

13. Lila has 10 books. She gives 4 books away.

book

4

Now Lila has | 6 | books.

10

14. Use the picture to write a story problem.
Write and solve the equation.

⬚ ◯ ⬚ = ⬚

⬚

_____
label

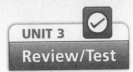
Solve the story problem.

15. Marty sees 8 birds at a feeder.
There are red birds and blue birds.
How many of each color bird can Marty see?
Show three correct answers.

bird

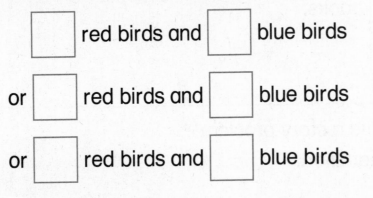

☐ red birds and ☐ blue birds

or ☐ red birds and ☐ blue birds

or ☐ red birds and ☐ blue birds

16. Read the story problem. Write a subtraction
and an addition equation for the story.
Draw a Math Mountain to match.

There are 7 leaves on the branch.
3 leaves fall off.
How many leaves are on the branch now?

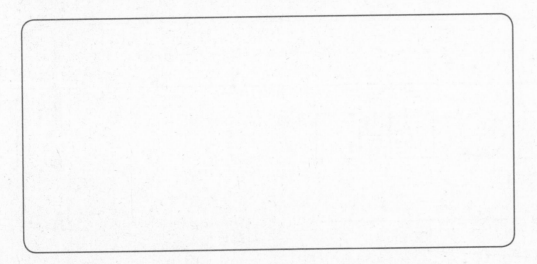

Dear Family:

Your child is learning about place value and numbers to 100. In this program, children begin by counting tens: 10, 20, 30, 40, and so on. They use a 10 × 10 Grid to help them "see" the relationship between the tens digit in a decade number and the number of tens it has.

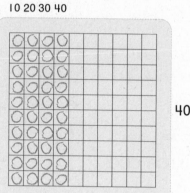

40 is 4 tens.

Soon, children will link 2-digit numbers to tens and extra ones. They will learn that a 2-digit number, such as 46, is made up of tens and ones, such as 40 and 6. Next, children will use what they know about adding 1-digit numbers to add 2-digit numbers.

$$3 + 4 = 7, \text{ so } 30 + 40 = 70.$$

Finally, they will learn to regroup and count on to find a total. For example:

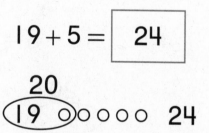

Right now, your child may enjoy counting by tens for you. He or she may also enjoy using household items to make groups of ten and extra ones, and then telling you the total number.

Sincerely,
Your child's teacher

 CA CC

Unit 4 addresses the following standards from the *Common Core State Standards for Mathematics with California Additions*: **1.OA.1, 1.OA.5, 1.OA.6, 1.NBT.1, 1.NBT.2, 1.NBT.2a, 1.NBT.2b, 1.NBT.2c, 1.NBT.3, 1.NBT.4,** and all Mathematical Practices.

Estimada familia:

Su niño está aprendiendo sobre valor posicional y los números hasta 100. En este programa, los niños empiezan contando decenas: 10, 20, 30, 40, etc. Usan una cuadrícula de 10 por 10 como ayuda para "ver" la relación entre el dígito de las decenas en el número que termina en cero y el número de decenas que tiene.

10 20 30 40

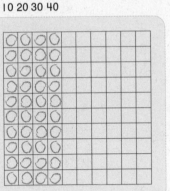

40 es 4 decenas.

En poco tiempo, los niños harán la conexión entre números de 2 dígitos y decenas más otras unidades. Aprenderán que un número de 2 dígitos, tal como 46, consta de decenas y unidades, como 40 y 6. Luego, los niños usarán lo que saben de la suma de números de 1 dígito para sumar números de 2 dígitos.

$$3 + 4 = 7, \text{ por lo tanto } 30 + 40 = 70.$$

Finalmente, aprenderán a reagrupar y contar hacia adelante para hallar el total. Por ejemplo:

$$19 + 5 = \boxed{24}$$

Por lo pronto, tal vez a su niño le guste contar en decenas para Ud. También puede gustarle usar objetos del hogar para formar grupos de diez más otras unidades y luego decir el número total.

Atentamente,
El maestro de su niño

 CA CC

En la Unidad 4 se aplican los siguientes estándares auxiliares, contenidos en los *Estándares estatales comunes de matemáticas con adiciones para California*: **1.OA.1, 1.OA.5, 1.OA.6, 1.NBT.1, 1.NBT.2, 1.NBT.2a, 1.NBT.2b, 1.NBT.2c, 1.NBT.3, 1.NBT.4** y todos los de prácticas matemáticas.

© Houghton Mifflin Harcourt Publishing Company

CA CC Content Standards **1.OA.5, 1.NBT.1, 1.NBT.2, 1.NBT.2a, 1.NBT.2c, 1.NBT.5**
Mathematical Practices **MP.2, MP.7**

How many circles? Count by **tens**.

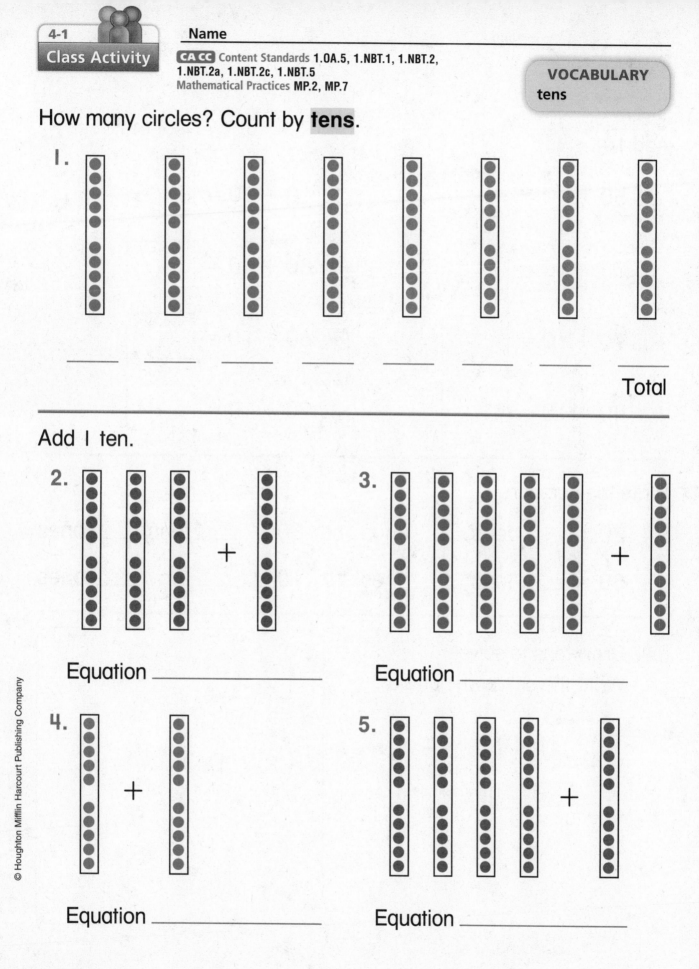

1.

_____ _____ _____ _____ _____ _____ _____ _____

Total

Add 1 ten.

2.

+

Equation _____

3.

+

Equation _____

4.

+

Equation _____

5.

+

Equation _____

Add 10.

6. $50 + 10 =$ ⬚   7. $10 + 10 =$ ⬚

8. $30 + 10 =$ ⬚   9. $80 + 10 =$ ⬚

10. $70 + 10 =$ ⬚   11. $60 + 10 =$ ⬚

12. $40 + 10 =$ ⬚   13. $90 + 10 =$ ⬚

Write the numbers.

14. $20 =$ ____ tens ____ ones   15. $80 =$ ____ tens ____ ones

16. $50 =$ ____ tens ____ ones   17. $10 =$ ____ ten ____ ones

18. Draw tens to solve.
    Write the unknown number.

    ⬚ $+ 10 = 30$

Introduction to Tens Groupings

Family Letter

Content Overview

Dear Family:

To help children "see" the tens and ones in 2-digit numbers, the *Math Expressions* program uses special drawings of 10-sticks to show tens, and circles to show ones. These images help children learn place value. Below are the numbers 27 and 52 shown with 10-sticks and circles:

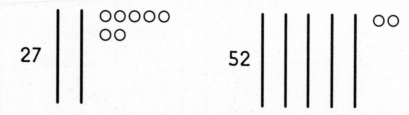

10-sticks and circles will also be used later to help children solve addition problems that require regrouping (sometimes called "carrying"). When there are enough circles to make a new ten, they are circled and then added like a 10-stick. The problem below shows 38 + 5:

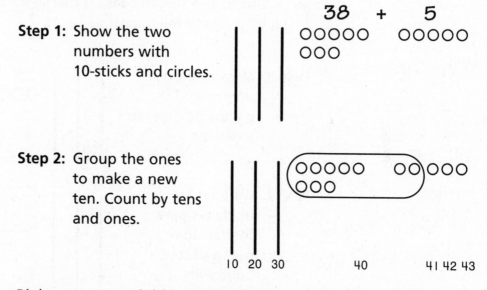

Step 1: Show the two numbers with 10-sticks and circles.

Step 2: Group the ones to make a new ten. Count by tens and ones.

Right now, your child is just beginning to show teen numbers with 10-sticks and circles. Soon your child will be able to draw 10-sticks and circles for any 2-digit number.

Sincerely,
Your child's teacher

CA CC

Unit 4 addresses the following standards from the *Common Core State Standards for Mathematics with California Additions*: 1.OA.1, 1.OA.5, 1.OA.6, 1.NBT.1, 1.NBT.2, 1.NBT.2a, 1.NBT.2b, 1.NBT.2c, 1.NBT.3, 1.NBT.4 and all Mathematical Practices.

Represent and Compare Teen Numbers **103**

Estimada familia:

Para ayudar a los niños a "ver" las decenas y las unidades en los números de 2 dígitos, el programa *Math Expressions* usa dibujos especiales de palitos de decenas para mostrar las decenas, y círculos para mostrar las unidades. Estas imágenes ayudan a los niños a aprender el valor posicional. Abajo se muestran los números 27 y 52 con palitos de decenas y círculos:

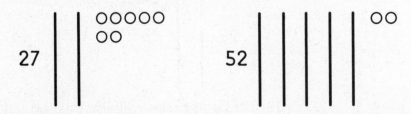

Más adelante, los palitos de decenas y los círculos también se usarán para ayudar a los niños a resolver problemas de suma que requieren reagrupar (que a veces se llama "llevar"). Cuando hay suficientes círculos para formar una nueva decena, se encierran en un círculo y se suman como si fueran un palito de decena. El siguiente problema muestra 38 + 5:

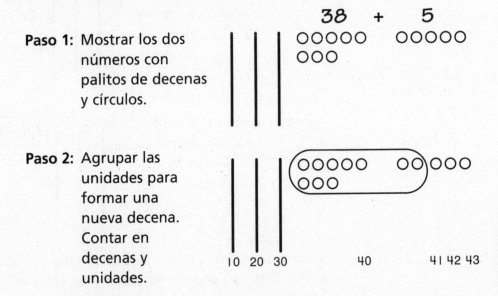

Paso 1: Mostrar los dos números con palitos de decenas y círculos.

Paso 2: Agrupar las unidades para formar una nueva decena. Contar en decenas y unidades.

Su niño está comenzando a mostrar los números de 11 a 19 con palitos de decenas y círculos. Pronto, podrá dibujar palitos de decenas y círculos para cualquier número de 2 dígitos.

Atentamente,
El maestro de su niño

© Houghton Mifflin Harcourt Publishing Company

CA CC

En la Unidad 4 se aplican los siguientes estándares auxiliares, contenidos en los *Estándares estatales comunes de matemáticas con adiciones para California*: 1.OA.1, 1.OA.5, 1.OA.6, 1.NBT.1, 1.NBT.2, 1.NBT.2a, 1.NBT.2b, 1.NBT.2c, 1.NBT.3, 1.NBT.4 y todos los de prácticas matemáticas.

1. Look at what Puzzled Penguin wrote.

$7 + 8 = 10 + \boxed{3}$

$7 + 8 = \boxed{13}$

Am I correct?

2. Help Puzzled Penguin.

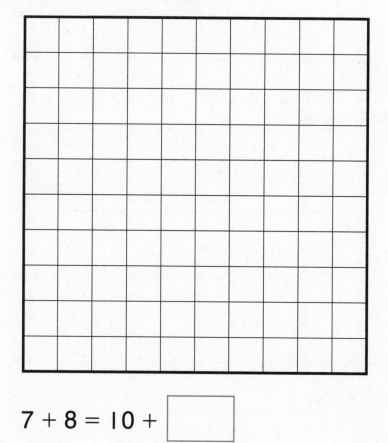

$7 + 8 = 10 + \boxed{}$

$7 + 8 = \boxed{}$

Find the total. Then **make a ten**.

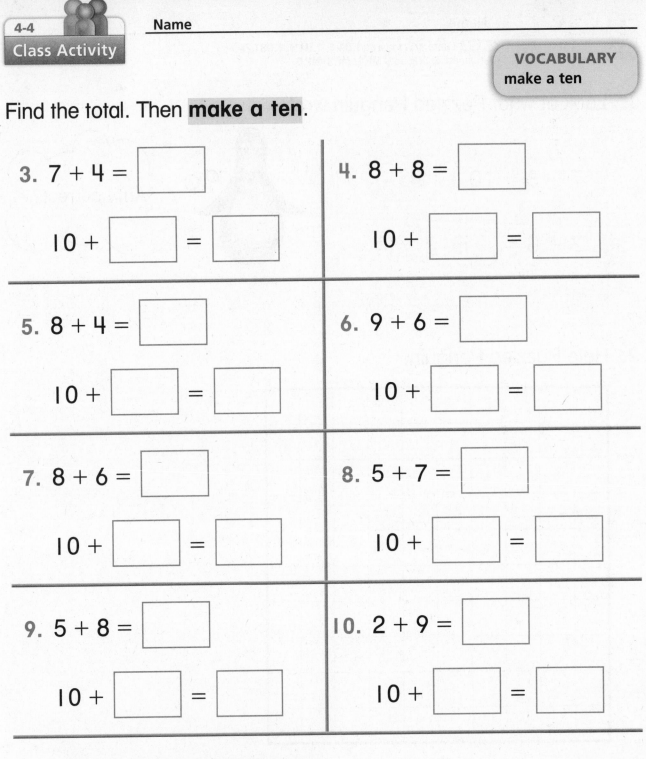

3. 7 + 4 = ☐

    10 + ☐ = ☐

4. 8 + 8 = ☐

    10 + ☐ = ☐

5. 8 + 4 = ☐

    10 + ☐ = ☐

6. 9 + 6 = ☐

    10 + ☐ = ☐

7. 8 + 6 = ☐

    10 + ☐ = ☐

8. 5 + 7 = ☐

    10 + ☐ = ☐

9. 5 + 8 = ☐

    10 + ☐ = ☐

10. 2 + 9 = ☐

    10 + ☐ = ☐

11. Write two equations that show
    different partners for 13.   _____
    Use 10 in one equation.
                                      _____

Visualize Teen Addition

5 + 7 = ☐

6 + 7 = ☐

9 + 9 = ☐

8 + 7 = ☐

9 + 7 = ☐

3 + 8 = ☐

4 + 8 = ☐

5 + 8 = ☐

6 + 8 = ☐

7 + 8 = ☐

8 + 8 = ☐

9 + 8 = ☐

3 + 9 = ☐

4 + 9 = ☐

5 + 9 = ☐

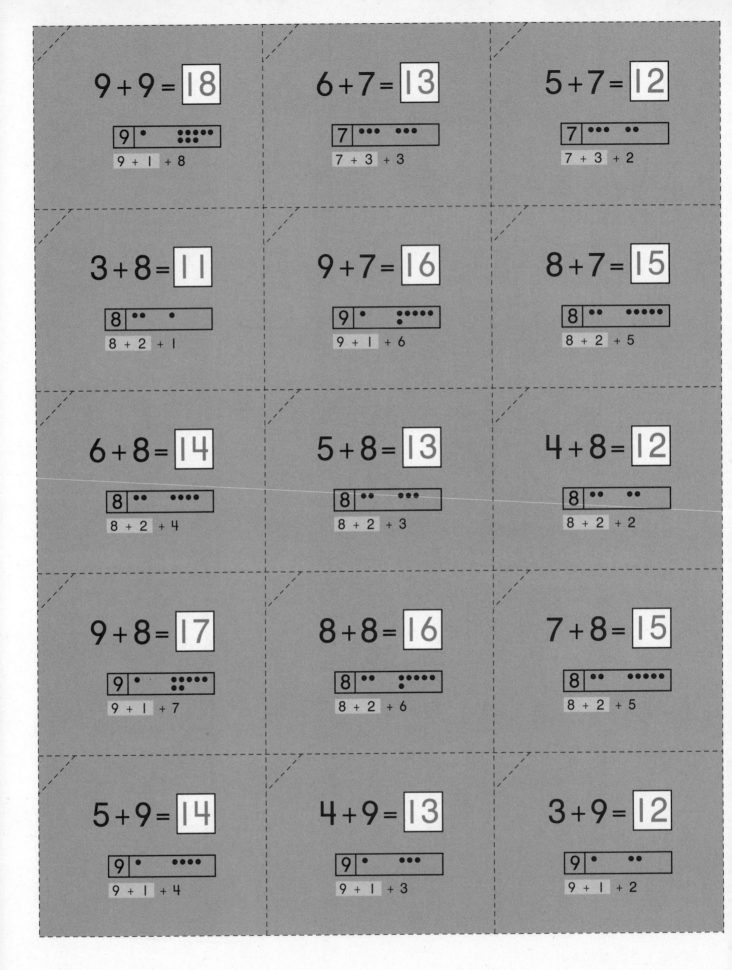

Green Make-a-Ten Cards

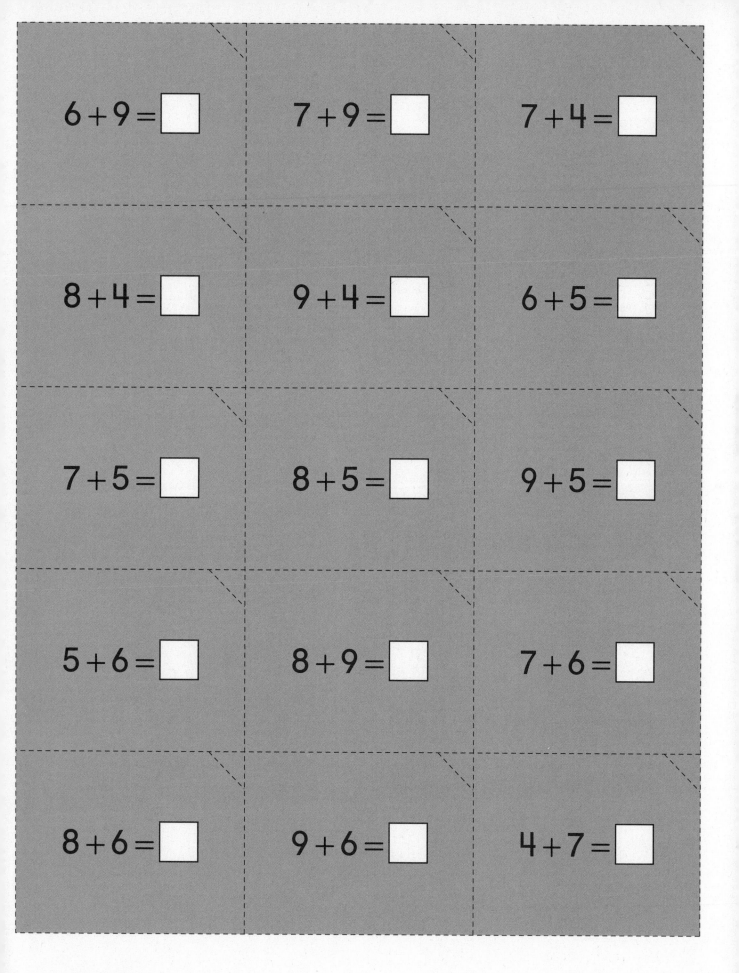

6 + 9 = ☐   7 + 9 = ☐   7 + 4 = ☐

8 + 4 = ☐   9 + 4 = ☐   6 + 5 = ☐

7 + 5 = ☐   8 + 5 = ☐   9 + 5 = ☐

5 + 6 = ☐   8 + 9 = ☐   7 + 6 = ☐

8 + 6 = ☐   9 + 6 = ☐   4 + 7 = ☐

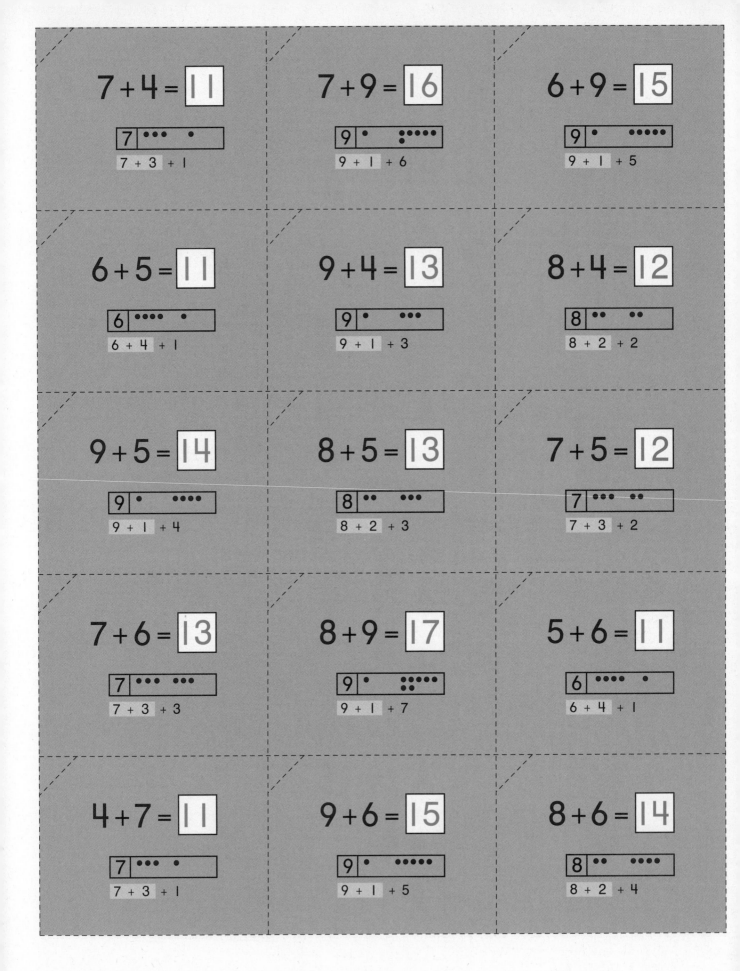

7 + 4 = 11
7 | ••• •
7 + 3 + 1

7 + 9 = 16
9 | • ••••
9 + 1 + 6

6 + 9 = 15
9 | • •••••
9 + 1 + 5

6 + 5 = 11
6 | •••• •
6 + 4 + 1

9 + 4 = 13
9 | • •••
9 + 1 + 3

8 + 4 = 12
8 | •• ••
8 + 2 + 2

9 + 5 = 14
9 | • ••••
9 + 1 + 4

8 + 5 = 13
8 | •• •••
8 + 2 + 3

7 + 5 = 12
7 | ••• ••
7 + 3 + 2

7 + 6 = 13
7 | ••• •••
7 + 3 + 3

8 + 9 = 17
9 | • •••••••
9 + 1 + 7

5 + 6 = 11
6 | •••• •
6 + 4 + 1

4 + 7 = 11
7 | ••• •
7 + 3 + 1

9 + 6 = 15
9 | • •••••
9 + 1 + 5

8 + 6 = 14
8 | •• ••••
8 + 2 + 4

Green Make-a-Ten Cards

Find the teen total.

1. 5 + 9 = ☐

2. 7 + 5 = ☐

3. 7 + 4 = ☐

4. 9 + 6 = ☐

5. 9 + 8 = ☐

6. 9 + 9 = ☐

7. 3 + 9 = ☐

8. 7 + 8 = ☐

9. 9 + 4 = ☐

10. 6 + 5 = ☐

11. 8 + 8 = ☐

12. 8 + 4 = ☐

13. 7 + 6 = ☐

14. 9 + 7 = ☐

15. Write an equation with a teen total.
Draw or explain how making a ten
can help you solve your equation.

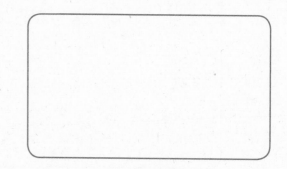

Find the total.

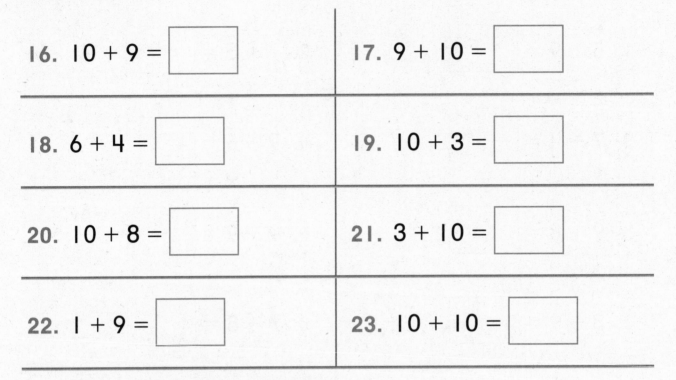

16. 10 + 9 = ☐

17. 9 + 10 = ☐

18. 6 + 4 = ☐

19. 10 + 3 = ☐

20. 10 + 8 = ☐

21. 3 + 10 = ☐

22. 1 + 9 = ☐

23. 10 + 10 = ☐

24. Draw or write to explain how you solved Exercise 23.

Teen Addition Strategies

Name

CA CC Content Standards **1.0A.6**
Mathematical Practices **MP.2, MP.7**

Use **doubles** to find the total.

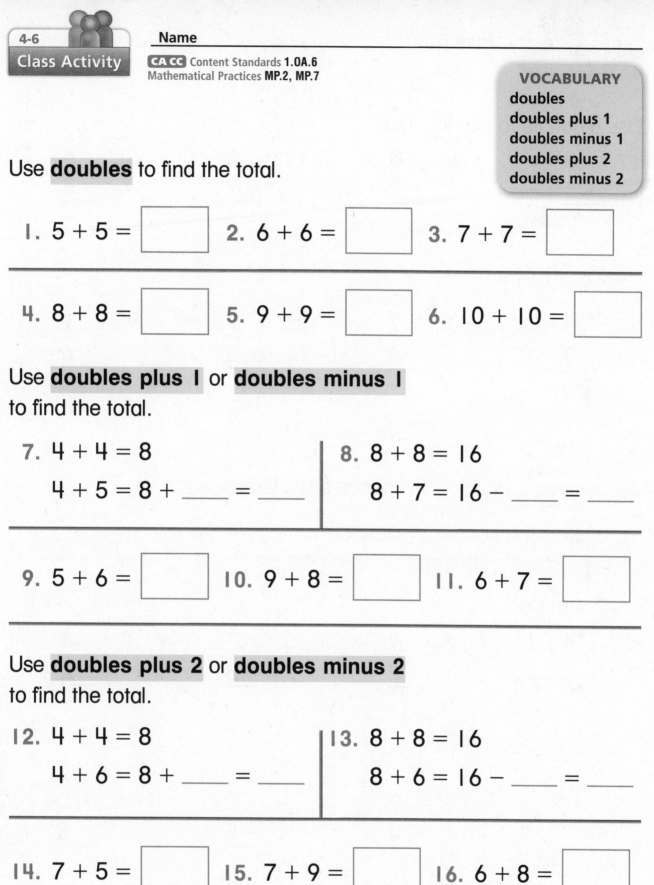

1. $5 + 5 =$ ☐   2. $6 + 6 =$ ☐   3. $7 + 7 =$ ☐

4. $8 + 8 =$ ☐   5. $9 + 9 =$ ☐   6. $10 + 10 =$ ☐

Use **doubles plus 1** or **doubles minus 1**
to find the total.

7. $4 + 4 = 8$
   $4 + 5 = 8 +$ ____ $=$ ____

8. $8 + 8 = 16$
   $8 + 7 = 16 -$ ____ $=$ ____

9. $5 + 6 =$ ☐   10. $9 + 8 =$ ☐   11. $6 + 7 =$ ☐

Use **doubles plus 2** or **doubles minus 2**
to find the total.

12. $4 + 4 = 8$
    $4 + 6 = 8 +$ ____ $=$ ____

13. $8 + 8 = 16$
    $8 + 6 = 16 -$ ____ $=$ ____

14. $7 + 5 =$ ☐   15. $7 + 9 =$ ☐   16. $6 + 8 =$ ☐

Use a double to find the total.

17.   8
    + 7

18.   10
    + 8

19.   5
    + 7

20.   6
    + 5

21.   8
    + 9

22.   7
    + 8

23.   7
    + 5

24.   7
    + 6

25. Write the double you used to solve Exercise 23.

_____

Subtract.

1.   6
   − 5

2.   9
   − 2

3.   7
   − 3

4.   8
   − 2

5.   10
   − 1

6.   9
   − 4

7.   8
   − 5

8.   10
   − 8

Investigate Doubles

1 one	11 eleven	10 ten
2 two	12 twelve	20 twenty
3 three	13 thirteen	30 thirty
4 four	14 fourteen	40 forty
5 five	15 fifteen	50 fifty
6 six	16 sixteen	60 sixty
7 seven	17 seventeen	70 seventy
8 eight	18 eighteen	80 eighty
9 nine	19 nineteen	90 ninety
10 ten	20 twenty	

Write the number.

1. five _____   fifteen _____   fifty _____

2. three _____   thirteen _____   thirty _____

3. two _____   twelve _____   twenty _____

4. sixty _____   sixteen _____   six _____

5. eighteen _____   eighty _____   eight _____

Write the number word.

6. 4 _____   14 _____   40 _____

7. 9 _____   19 _____   90 _____

8. 2 _____   12 _____   20 _____

9. 70 _____   17 _____   7 _____

10. 1 _____   10 _____   11 _____

1 one	11 eleven	10 ten
2 two	12 twelve	20 twenty
3 three	13 thirteen	30 thirty
4 four	14 fourteen	40 forty
5 five	15 fifteen	50 fifty
6 six	16 sixteen	60 sixty
7 seven	17 seventeen	70 seventy
8 eight	18 eighteen	80 eighty
9 nine	19 nineteen	90 ninety

Write the number word.

11. | ○○ _____

12. | | | _____

13. | ○○○ _____

14. ○○○ _____

15. | | | | | | _____

16. | ○○○○○ _____

17. Write the numbers 1–20.

1									
									20

18. Write the decade numbers 10–90.

10	20							

Integrate Tens and Ones

Each box has 10 muffins. How many muffins are there?

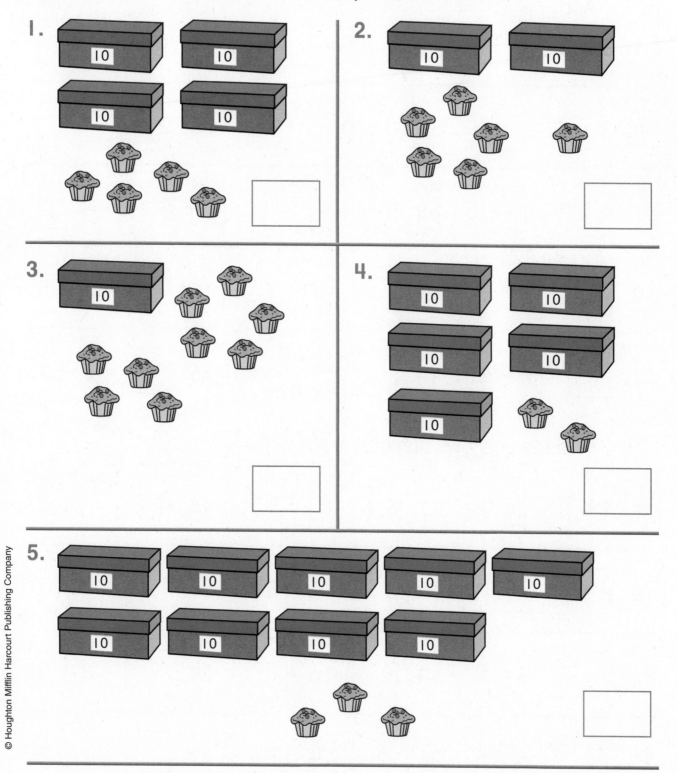

6. **Discuss** How are 23 and 32 the same? How are they different?

PATH to FLUENCY **Add.**

1. $3 + 3 =$ ☐

2. $4 + 5 =$ ☐

3. $1 + 5 =$ ☐

4. $3 + 7 =$ ☐

5. $8 + 0 =$ ☐

6. $2 + 5 =$ ☐

7. $4 + 2 =$ ☐

8. $4 + 4 =$ ☐

9. $3 + 6 =$ ☐

10. ☐ $= 5 + 2$

11. ☐ $= 7 + 1$

12. ☐ $= 5 + 5$

13. ☐ $= 1 + 6$

14. ☐ $= 7 + 3$

15. ☐ $= 5 + 3$

PATH to FLUENCY **Find the unknown number.**

16. $2 +$ ☐ $= 9$

17. $6 +$ ☐ $= 10$

18. $4 +$ ☐ $= 7$

19. $8 +$ ☐ $= 10$

20. $3 +$ ☐ $= 8$

21. $1 +$ ☐ $= 10$

22. ☐ $+ 3 = 9$

23. ☐ $+ 6 = 8$

24. ☐ $+ 8 = 9$

25. ☐ $+ 6 = 6$

26. ☐ $+ 4 = 7$

27. ☐ $+ 2 = 9$

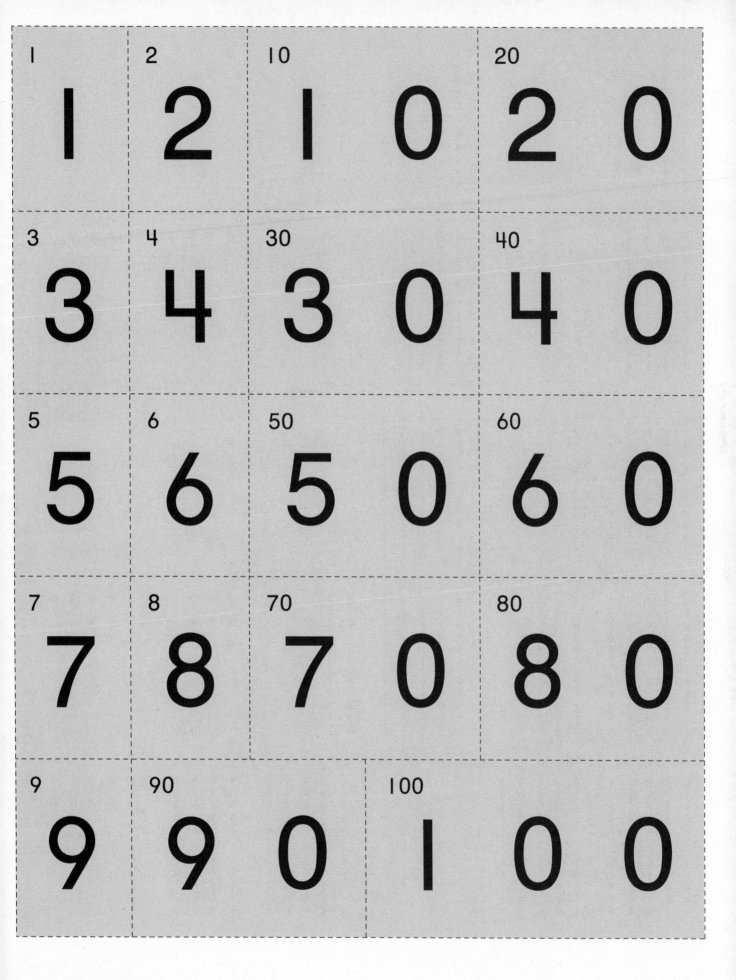

Secret Code Cards

Name _____

CA CC Content Standards 1.NBT.2, 1.NBT.3
Mathematical Practices MP.2, MP.3, MP.6

> [!NOTE]
> **VOCABULARY**
> compare

Compare the numbers. Write >, <, or =.

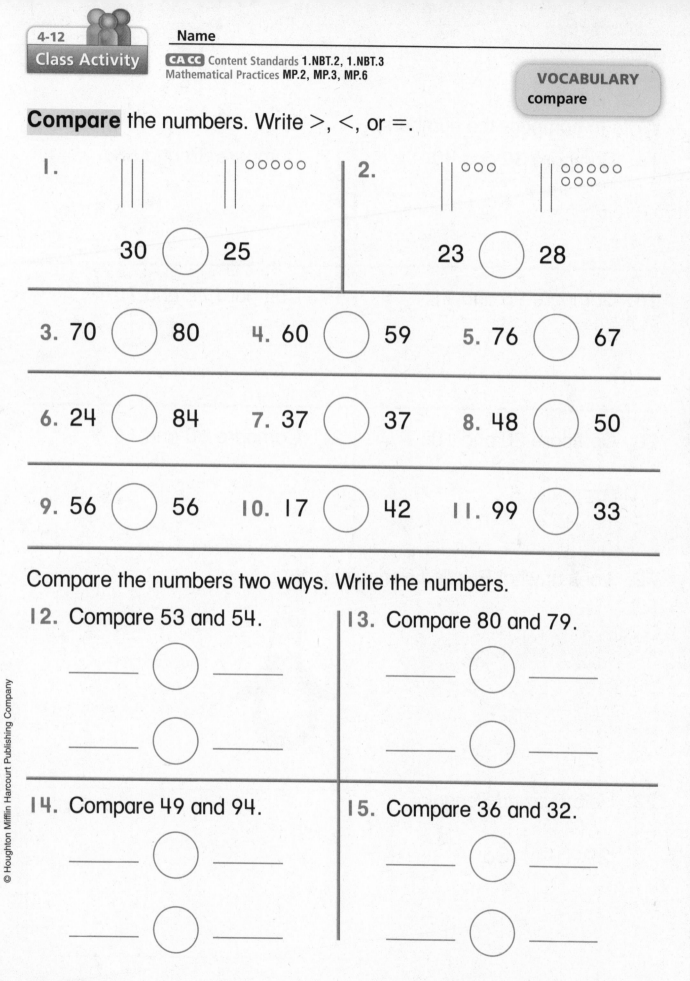

1. 30 ◯ 25

2. 23 ◯ 28

3. 70 ◯ 80   4. 60 ◯ 59   5. 76 ◯ 67

6. 24 ◯ 84   7. 37 ◯ 37   8. 48 ◯ 50

9. 56 ◯ 56   10. 17 ◯ 42   11. 99 ◯ 33

Compare the numbers two ways. Write the numbers.

12. Compare 53 and 54.

____ ◯ ____

____ ◯ ____

13. Compare 80 and 79.

____ ◯ ____

____ ◯ ____

14. Compare 49 and 94.

____ ◯ ____

____ ◯ ____

15. Compare 36 and 32.

____ ◯ ____

____ ◯ ____

Write to compare the numbers.

16. Compare 39 and 40.

_____ ◯ _____

17. Compare 86 and 68.

_____ ◯ _____

18. Compare 95 and 91.

_____ ◯ _____

19. Compare 72 and 72.

_____ ◯ _____

20. Compare 20 and 10.

_____ ◯ _____

21. Compare 60 and 16.

_____ ◯ _____

22. Look at what Puzzled Penguin wrote.

29 ◯ > ◯ 36

Am I correct?

23. Help Puzzled Penguin.

29 ◯ 36

Use Place Value to Compare Numbers

Solve.

1. $3 + 6 =$ _____

    $30 + 60 =$ _____

    $30 + 6 =$ _____

2. $4 + 5 =$ _____

    $40 + 50 =$ _____

    $40 + 5 =$ _____

3. $2 + 4 =$ _____

    $20 + 40 =$ _____

    $20 + 4 =$ _____

4. $5 + 2 =$ _____

    $50 + 20 =$ _____

    $50 + 2 =$ _____

5. $7 + 2 =$ _____

    $70 + 20 =$ _____

    $70 + 2 =$ _____

6. $4 + 1 =$ _____

    $40 + 10 =$ _____

    $40 + 1 =$ _____

7. $3 + 2 =$ _____

    $30 + 20 =$ _____

    $30 + 2 =$ _____

8. $1 + 8 =$ _____

    $10 + 80 =$ _____

    $10 + 8 =$ _____

Complete the set of equations to follow the
same rules as each set above. Then solve.

9. $3 + 5 =$ _____

    $30 +$ _____ $=$ _____

    $30 +$ _____ $=$ _____

10. $4 + 3 =$ _____

    $40 +$ _____ $=$ _____

    $40 +$ _____ $=$ _____

Class Activity

Name _____

Find the unknown numbers to complete
the set of equations.

11. $2 +$ _____ $= 5$

    $20 + 30 =$ _____

    $20 +$ _____ $= 23$

12. $4 +$ _____ $= 8$

    _____ $+ 40 = 80$

    $40 + 4 =$ _____

13. _____ $+ 2 = 6$

    $40 +$ _____ $= 60$

    _____ $+ 2 = 42$

14. _____ $+ 7 = 8$

    $10 +$ _____ $= 80$

    $10 + 7 =$ _____

15. Look at what Puzzled Penguin wrote.

$50 + 4 = \boxed{90}$

Am I correct?

16. Help Puzzled Penguin.

$50 + 4 = \boxed{}$

Mixed Addition with Tens and Ones

Name

CA CC Content Standards **1.OA.6, 1.NBT.4**
Mathematical Practices **MP.2**

Here is a riddle.

> I like to hop,
> but my ears are small.
> I have four legs, but I stand tall.
> I have a pocket,
> but I cannot buy.
> Guess my name. Who am I?

Find the total. Use any method.

1. $46 + 5 =$ ☐ O

2. $40 + 2 =$ ☐ O

3. $12 + 7 =$ ☐ K

4. $29 + 5 =$ ☐ R

5. $64 + 6 =$ ☐ A

6. $20 + 9 =$ ☐ A

7. $27 + 5 =$ ☐ G

8. $89 + 2 =$ ☐ N

Who am I? Write the letter for each total.

___ ___ ___ ___ ___ ___ ___ ___
19   70   91   32   29   34   42   51

PATH to FLUENCY Add.

1. $4 + 5 =$ ☐ 2. $0 + 7 =$ ☐ 3. $7 + 3 =$ ☐

4. $1 + 6 =$ ☐ 5. $6 + 2 =$ ☐ 6. $4 + 2 =$ ☐

7. $5 + 5 =$ ☐ 8. $9 + 1 =$ ☐ 9. $2 + 5 =$ ☐

10. ☐ $= 7 + 1$ 11. ☐ $= 3 + 6$ 12. ☐ $= 7 + 2$

13. ☐ $= 6 + 4$ 14. ☐ $= 2 + 4$ 15. ☐ $= 4 + 3$

PATH to FLUENCY Find the unknown number.

16. $1 +$ ☐ $= 8$ 17. $3 +$ ☐ $= 7$ 18. $5 +$ ☐ $= 8$

19. $8 +$ ☐ $= 10$ 20. $4 +$ ☐ $= 8$ 21. $9 +$ ☐ $= 9$

22. ☐ $+ 1 = 6$ 23. ☐ $+ 4 = 9$ 24. ☐ $+ 7 = 10$

25. ☐ $+ 8 = 9$ 26. ☐ $+ 5 = 8$ 27. ☐ $+ 8 = 10$

Counting On Strategy: 2-Digit Numbers

CA CC Content Standards **1.NBT.1, 1.NBT.3, 1.NBT.4**
Mathematical Practices **MP.2, MP.5**

Use this sandwich sheet when you play
The Sandwich Game.

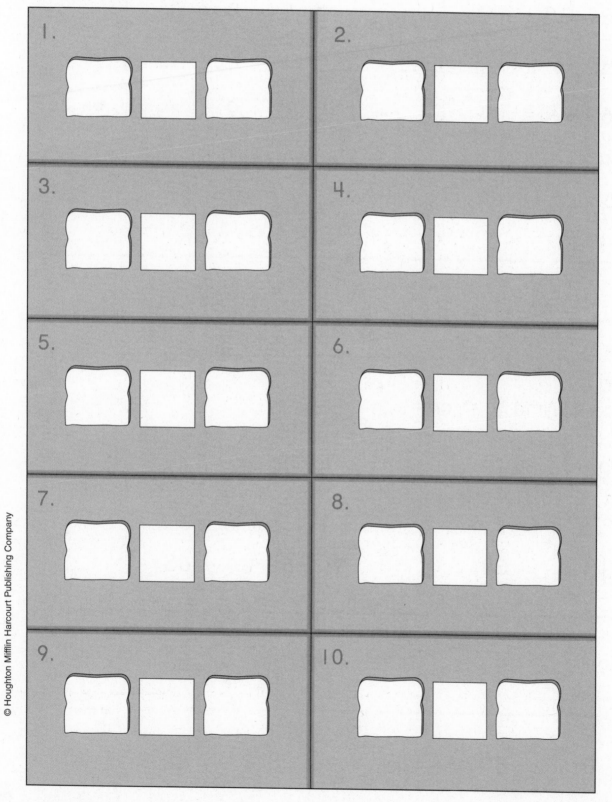

Find the total. Use any method.

11. $29 + 3 = $ ⬚

12. $11 + 8 = $ ⬚

13. $67 + 4 = $ ⬚

14. $33 + 9 = $ ⬚

15. $96 + 3 = $ ⬚

16. $46 + 4 = $ ⬚

17. $12 + 8 = $ ⬚

18. $71 + 5 = $ ⬚

Compare. Write >, <, or =.

19. 26 ◯ 62

20. 80 ◯ 79

21. 18 ◯ 38

22. 65 ◯ 65

23. 97 ◯ 94

24. 45 ◯ 53

25. 8 ◯ 80

26. 23 ◯ 22

Practice with 2-Digit Numbers

CA CC Content Standards **1.NBT.1, 1.NBT.2, 1.NBT.3**
Mathematical Practices **MP.1, MP.2, MP.6**

► **Math and the Community Theater**

Linda and her family go to a show.

1. 10 cars can park in each row.

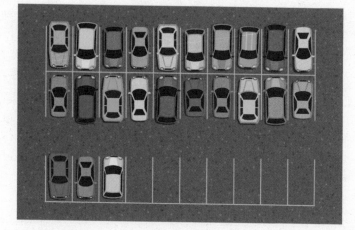

How many cars are there?

_____ tens _____ ones = _____ cars

2. 10 people can sit in each row.

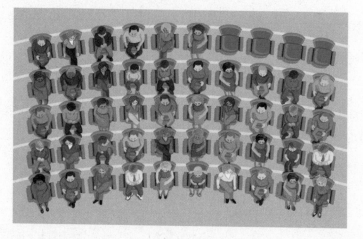

How many people are there?

_____ tens _____ ones = _____ people

Name _____

Show tickets were sold on Friday, Saturday, and Sunday.

3. Write the number of tickets sold each day.

Friday	![tickets and ADMIT ONE tickets]
	_____ tens _____ ones = _____ tickets
Saturday	![tickets and ADMIT ONE tickets]
	_____ tens _____ ones = _____ tickets
Sunday	![tickets and ADMIT ONE tickets]
	_____ tens _____ ones = _____ tickets

Compare the number of tickets sold.
Use >, <, or =.

4. Friday   Saturday

    [ ]   ◯   [ ]

5. Friday   Sunday

    [ ]   ◯   [ ]

6. Saturday   Sunday

    [ ]   ◯   [ ]

7. Sunday   Saturday

    [ ]   ◯   [ ]

Focus on Mathematical Practices

1. Does the number match the picture?
Choose Yes or No.

| | | | | | 50

○ Yes   ○ No

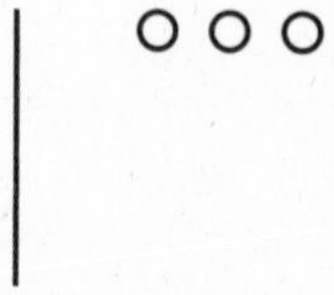

| ○ ○ ○

31

○ Yes   ○ No

Draw 10-sticks and circles.
Write how many tens and ones.

2.   32

[ ] tens [ ] ones = 32

3.   64

[ ] tens [ ] ones = 64

Use the words on the tiles to name each number.

| seventy | seven | seventeen |

4. 17 _____

5. 70 _____

6. 7 _____

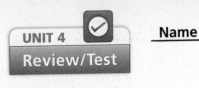
7. Add 1 ten.

$$30 + 10 = \boxed{}$$

8. How many paper clips?

$$\boxed{}$$

9. Draw a picture for the problem.
Write an equation to solve.

There are 10 birds in one tree.
There are 7 birds in another tree.
How many birds are there?

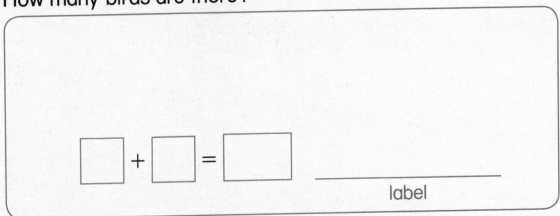

$$\boxed{} + \boxed{} = \boxed{}$$
_____
label

How many cupcakes are there?

10.

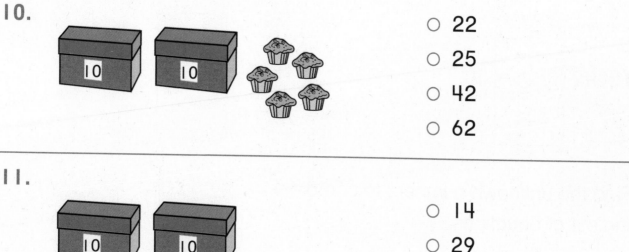

○ 22
○ 25
○ 42
○ 62

11.

○ 14
○ 29
○ 31
○ 41

Solve the story problem.

12. Kimi has 8 red apples and
5 green apples. How many
apples does she have?

apple

[   ] _____
          label

13. Hector has a box of 4 red pencils
and 7 blue pencils. How many
pencils does he have?

box

[   ] _____
          label

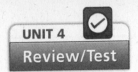
Name _____

Ring >, <, or = to compare the numbers.

14. 42 | > / < / = | 50

15. 34 | > / < / = | 33

Find the unknown numbers to complete
the set of equations.

16. $3 + \underline{\hspace{1cm}} = 7$

$30 + 40 = \underline{\hspace{1cm}}$

$30 + \underline{\hspace{1cm}} = 34$

17. $\underline{\hspace{1cm}} + 7 = 9$

$20 + \underline{\hspace{1cm}} = 90$

$20 + 7 = \underline{\hspace{1cm}}$

18. Write a number from 10 to 40.
Add 1 ten. Write the new number.
Draw and write to compare the numbers.

Problem Types

	Result Unknown	Change Unknown	Start Unknown
Add To	Six children are playing tag in the yard. Three more children come to play. How many children are playing in the yard now? *Situation and Solution Equation*[1]*:* $6 + 3 = \square$	Six children are playing tag in the yard. Some more children come to play. Now there are 9 children in the yard. How many children came to play? *Situation Equation:* $6 + \square = 9$ *Solution Equation:* $9 - 6 = \square$	Some children are playing tag in the yard. Three more children come to play. Now there are 9 children in the yard. How many children were in the yard at first? *Situation Equation:* $\square + 3 = 9$ *Solution Equation:* $9 - 3 = \square$
Take From	Jake has 10 trading cards. He gives 3 to his brother. How many trading cards does he have left? *Situation and Solution Equation:* $10 - 3 = \square$	Jake has 10 trading cards. He gives some to his brother. Now Jake has 7 trading cards left. How many cards does he give to his brother? *Situation Equation:* $10 - \square = 7$ *Solution Equation:* $10 - 7 = \square$	Jake has some trading cards. He gives 3 to his brother. Now Jake has 7 trading cards left. How many cards does he start with? *Situation Equation:* $\square - 3 = 7$ *Solution Equation:* $7 + 3 = \square$

[1]A situation equation represents the structure (action) in the problem situation. A solution equation shows the operation used to find the answer.

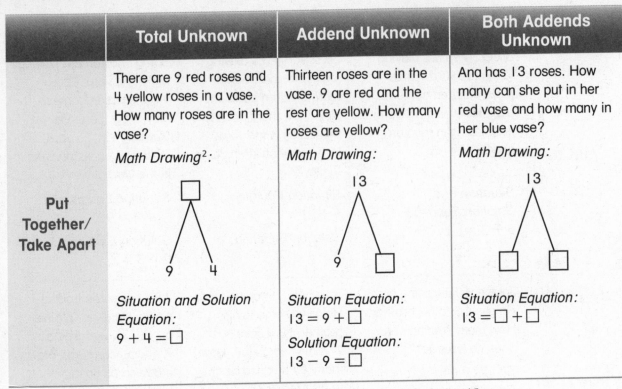

	Total Unknown	Addend Unknown	Both Addends Unknown
Put Together/ Take Apart	There are 9 red roses and 4 yellow roses in a vase. How many roses are in the vase?	Thirteen roses are in the vase. 9 are red and the rest are yellow. How many roses are yellow?	Ana has 13 roses. How many can she put in her red vase and how many in her blue vase?

*These math drawings are called Math Mountains in Grades 1–3 and break-apart drawings in Grades 4 and 5.

Total Unknown

Math Drawing²:

Situation and Solution Equation:
$9 + 4 = \square$

Addend Unknown

Math Drawing:

Situation Equation:
$13 = 9 + \square$

Solution Equation:
$13 - 9 = \square$

Both Addends Unknown

Math Drawing:

Situation Equation:
$13 = \square + \square$

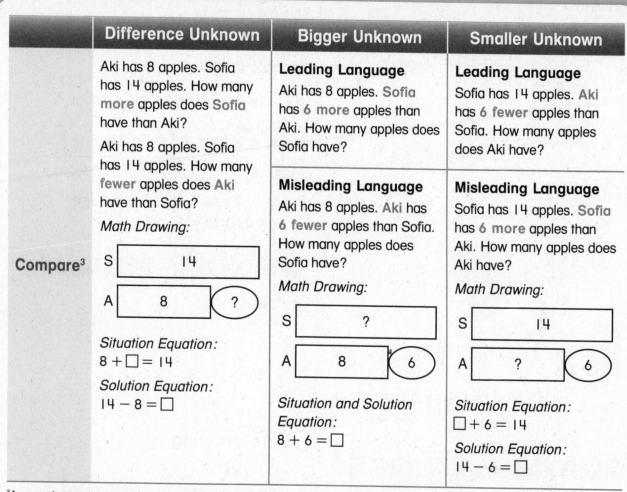

Difference Unknown	Bigger Unknown	Smaller Unknown
Compare[3]		

Difference Unknown

Aki has 8 apples. Sofia has 14 apples. How many **more** apples does **Sofia** have than Aki?

Aki has 8 apples. Sofia has 14 apples. How many **fewer** apples does **Aki** have than Sofia?

Math Drawing:

S [14]

A [8] (?)

Situation Equation:
8 + □ = 14

Solution Equation:
14 − 8 = □

Bigger Unknown

Leading Language

Aki has 8 apples. **Sofia** has **6 more** apples than Aki. How many apples does Sofia have?

Misleading Language

Aki has 8 apples. **Aki** has **6 fewer** apples than Sofia. How many apples does Sofia have?

Math Drawing:

S [?]

A [8] (6)

Situation and Solution Equation:
8 + 6 = □

Smaller Unknown

Leading Language

Sofia has 14 apples. **Aki** has **6 fewer** apples than Sofia. How many apples does Aki have?

Misleading Language

Sofia has 14 apples. **Sofia** has **6 more** apples than Aki. How many apples does Aki have?

Math Drawing:

S [14]

A [?] (6)

Situation Equation:
□ + 6 = 14

Solution Equation:
14 − 6 = □

[3]A comparison sentence can always be said in two ways. One way uses *more*, and the other uses *fewer* or *less*. Misleading language suggests the wrong operation. For example, it says *Aki has 6 fewer apples than Sofia*, but you have to add 6 to Aki's 8 apples to get 14 apples.

Glossary

5-group

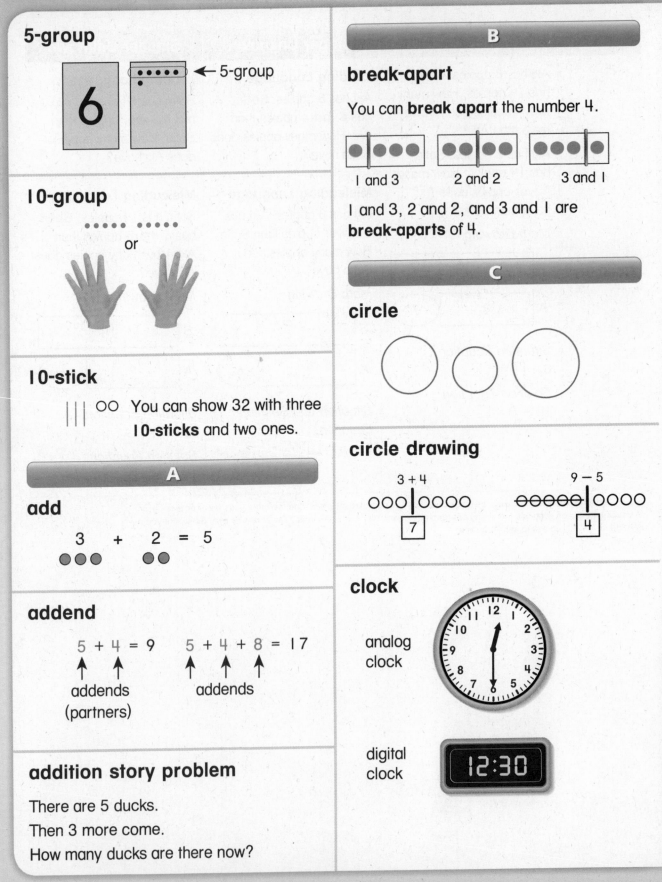

← 5-group

6

10-group

....

or

10-stick

||| OO You can show 32 with three **10-sticks** and two ones.

A

add

3 + 2 = 5

●●● ●●

addend

5 + 4 = 9   5 + 4 + 8 = 17

↑   ↑   ↑   ↑   ↑

addends   addends
(partners)

addition story problem

There are 5 ducks.

Then 3 more come.

How many ducks are there now?

B

break-apart

You can **break apart** the number 4.

●|●●●   ●●|●●   ●●●|●

1 and 3   2 and 2   3 and 1

1 and 3, 2 and 2, and 3 and 1 are
break-aparts of 4.

C

circle

circle drawing

3 + 4   9 − 5

OOO|OOOO   OⒺOⒺO|OOOO

7   4

clock

analog
clock

digital
clock

12:30

© Houghton Mifflin Harcourt Publishing Company

column

1	11	21	31	41	51	61	71	81	91
2	12	22	32	42	52	62	72	82	92
3	13	23	33	43	53	63	73	83	93
4	14	24	34	44	54	64	74	84	94
5	15	25	35	45	55	65	75	85	95
6	16	26	36	46	56	66	76	86	96
7	17	27	37	47	57	67	77	87	97
8	18	28	38	48	58	68	78	88	98
9	19	29	39	49	59	69	79	89	99
10	20	30	40	50	60	70	80	90	100

compare

You can **compare** numbers.

11 is less than 12.

$11 < 12$

12 is greater than 11.

$12 > 11$

You can **compare** objects by length.

The crayon is shorter than the pencil.

The pencil is longer than the crayon.

comparison bars

Joe has 6 roses. Sasha has 9 roses. How many more roses does Sasha have than Joe?

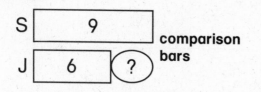

comparison bars

cone

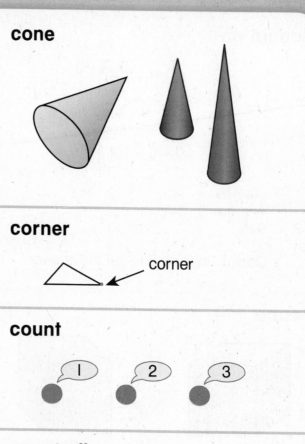

corner

corner

count

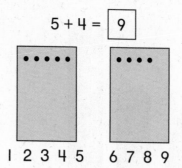

count all

$5 + 4 = \boxed{9}$

1 2 3 4 5   6 7 8 9

count on

$$5 + 4 = \boxed{9}$$

$$5 + \boxed{4} = 9$$

$$9 - 5 = \boxed{4}$$

5 $\overset{\bullet\ \ \bullet\ \ \bullet\ \ \bullet}{6\ 7\ 8\ 9}$

Count on from 5 to get the answer.

cube

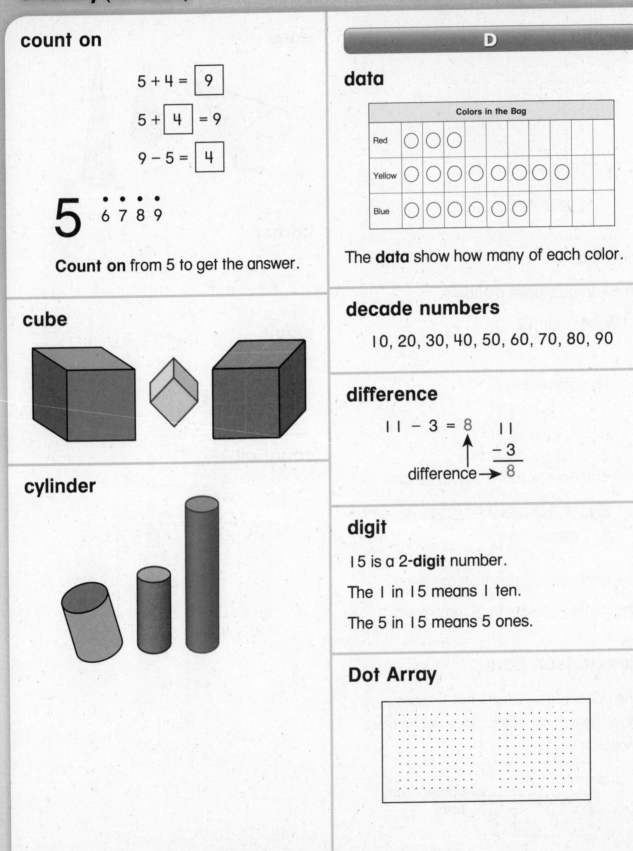

cylinder

D

data

Colors in the Bag								
Red	◯	◯	◯					
Yellow	◯	◯	◯	◯	◯	◯	◯	◯
Blue	◯	◯	◯	◯	◯	◯		

The **data** show how many of each color.

decade numbers

10, 20, 30, 40, 50, 60, 70, 80, 90

difference

$$11 - 3 = 8 \qquad \begin{array}{r} 11 \\ -\ 3 \\ \hline 8 \end{array}$$

difference → 8

digit

15 is a 2-**digit** number.

The 1 in 15 means 1 ten.

The 5 in 15 means 5 ones.

Dot Array

doubles

$$4 + 4 = 8$$

Both partners are the same.
They are **doubles**.

doubles minus 1

$7 + 7 = 14$, so

$7 + 6 = 13$, 1 less than 14.

doubles minus 2

$7 + 7 = 14$, so

$7 + 5 = 12$, 2 less than 14.

doubles plus 1

$6 + 6 = 12$, so

$6 + 7 = 13$, 1 more than 12.

doubles plus 2

$6 + 6 = 12$, so

$6 + 8 = 14$, 2 more than 12.

E

edge

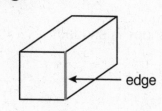

edge

equal shares

2 equal shares   4 equal shares

These show **equal shares**.

equal to (=)

$$4 + 4 = 8$$

4 plus 4 is **equal to** 8.

equation

Examples:

$4 + 3 = 7$ $7 = 4 + 3$

$9 - 5 = 4$ $4 = 9 - 5$

F

face

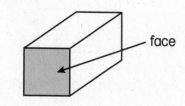

face

fewer

Eggs Laid This Month

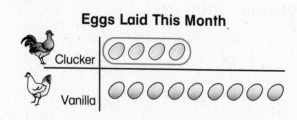

Clucker laid **fewer** eggs than Vanilla.

fewest

Eggs Laid This Month

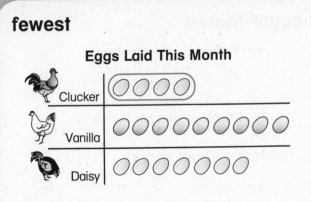

Clucker laid the **fewest** eggs.

fourth of

One **fourth of** the shape is shaded.

fourths

I whole   4 **fourths**, or 4 quarters

G

greater than (>)

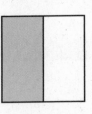

34   >   25

34 is greater than 25.

grid

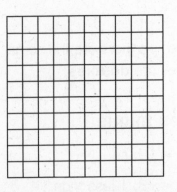

H

half-hour

minute hand

A **half-hour** is 30 minutes.

half of

One **half of** the shape is shaded.

halves

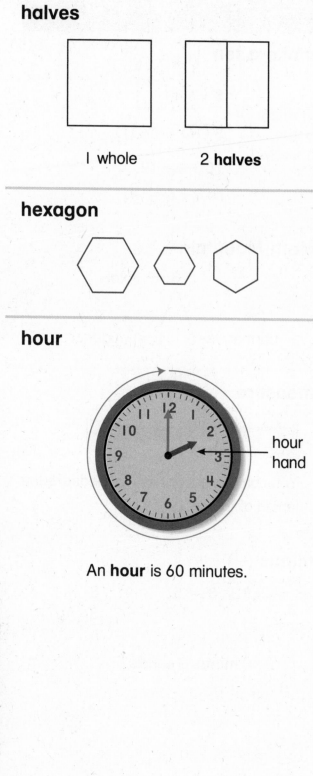

1 whole   2 **halves**

hexagon

hour

An **hour** is 60 minutes.

hour hand

hundred

1	11	21	31	41	51	61	71	81	91
2	12	22	32	42	52	62	72	82	92
3	13	23	33	43	53	63	73	83	93
4	14	24	34	44	54	64	74	84	94
5	15	25	35	45	55	65	75	85	95
6	16	26	36	46	56	66	76	86	96
7	17	27	37	47	57	67	77	87	97
8	18	28	38	48	58	68	78	88	98
9	19	29	39	49	59	69	79	89	99
10	20	30	40	50	60	70	80	90	100

or

K

known partner

$5 + \boxed{} = 7$

5 is the **known partner**.

L

label

We see 9 fish.

5 are big. The others are small.

How many fish are small?

4   fish
      label

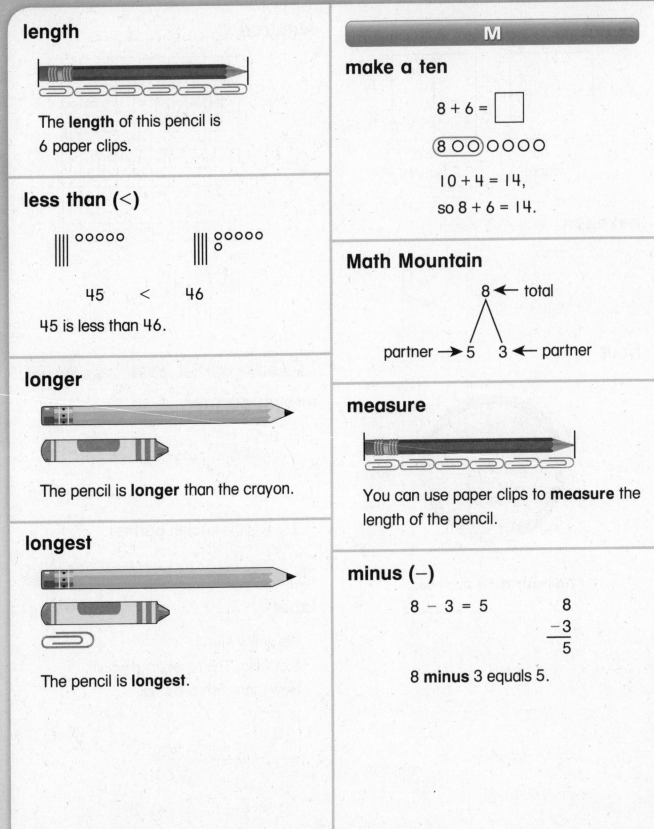

length

The **length** of this pencil is
6 paper clips.

less than (<)

45   <   46

45 is less than 46.

longer

The pencil is **longer** than the crayon.

longest

The pencil is **longest**.

M

make a ten

$8 + 6 = \square$

$10 + 4 = 14$,
so $8 + 6 = 14$.

Math Mountain

8 ← total

partner → 5   3 ← partner

measure

You can use paper clips to **measure** the
length of the pencil.

minus (−)

$$8 - 3 = 5 \qquad \begin{array}{r} 8 \\ -3 \\ \hline 5 \end{array}$$

8 **minus** 3 equals 5.

minute

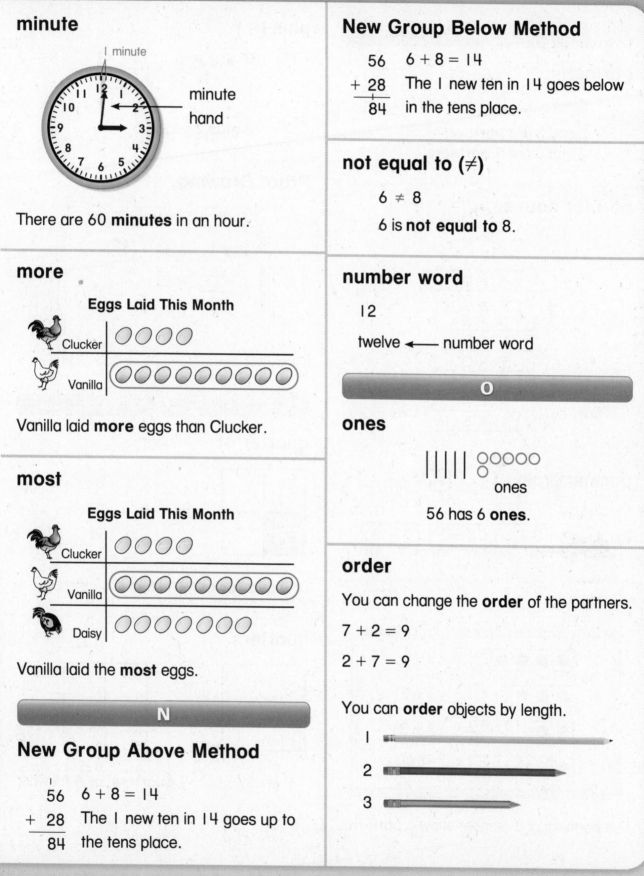

I minute

minute hand

There are 60 **minutes** in an hour.

more

Eggs Laid This Month

Clucker | ⬭⬭⬭⬭

Vanilla | ⬭⬭⬭⬭⬭⬭⬭⬭⬭⬭

Vanilla laid **more** eggs than Clucker.

most

Eggs Laid This Month

Clucker | ⬭⬭⬭⬭

Vanilla | ⬭⬭⬭⬭⬭⬭⬭⬭⬭

Daisy | ⬭⬭⬭⬭⬭⬭⬭

Vanilla laid the **most** eggs.

N

New Group Above Method

$$\begin{array}{r} \overset{1}{56} \\ + 28 \\ \hline 84 \end{array}$$ 6 + 8 = 14

The 1 new ten in 14 goes up to the tens place.

New Group Below Method

$$\begin{array}{r} 56 \\ + 28 \\ \hline 84 \end{array}$$ 6 + 8 = 14

The 1 new ten in 14 goes below in the tens place.

not equal to ($\neq$)

6 $\neq$ 8

6 is **not equal to** 8.

number word

12

twelve ← number word

O

ones

||||| ○○○○○

ones

56 has 6 **ones**.

order

You can change the **order** of the partners.

7 + 2 = 9

2 + 7 = 9

You can **order** objects by length.

1
2
3

P

partner

$5 = 2 + 3$

2 and 3 are **partners** of 5.
2 and 3 are 5-**partners**.

partner house

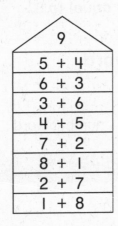

partner train

4-train

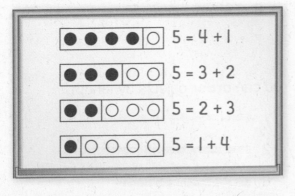

pattern

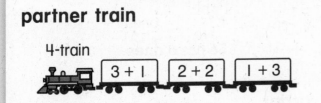

The partners of a number show a **pattern**.

plus (+)

$3 + 2 = 5$

$$\begin{array}{r} 3 \\ + 2 \\ \hline 5 \end{array}$$

3 **plus** 2 equals 5.

Proof Drawing

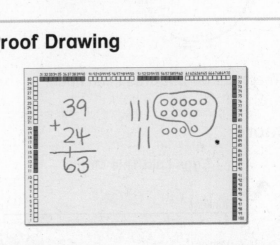

Q

quarter of

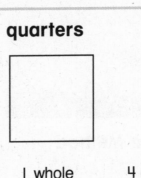

One **quarter of** the shape is shaded.

quarters

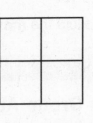

1 whole   4 **quarters**, or 4 fourths

R

rectangle

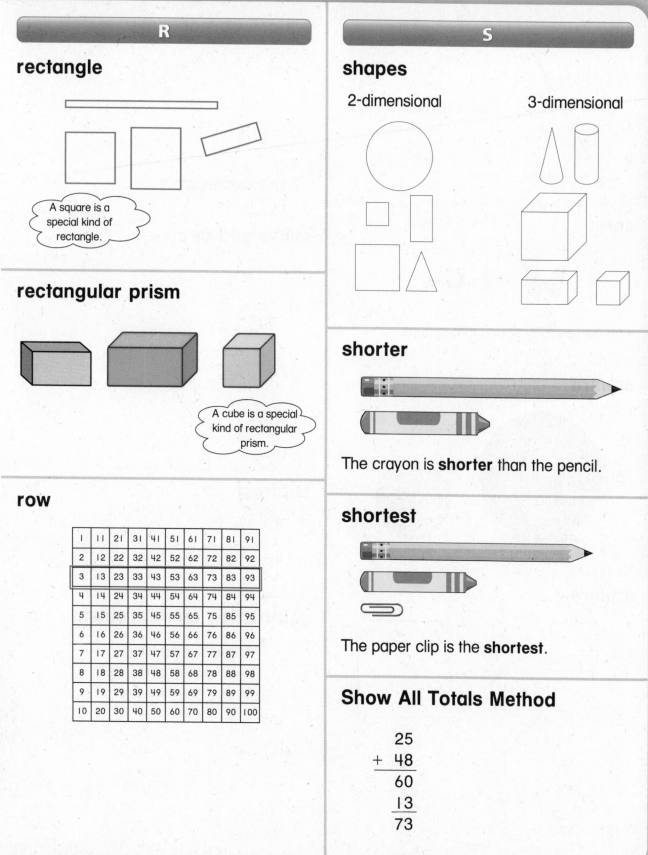

A square is a special kind of rectangle.

rectangular prism

A cube is a special kind of rectangular prism.

row

1	11	21	31	41	51	61	71	81	91
2	12	22	32	42	52	62	72	82	92
3	13	23	33	43	53	63	73	83	93
4	14	24	34	44	54	64	74	84	94
5	15	25	35	45	55	65	75	85	95
6	16	26	36	46	56	66	76	86	96
7	17	27	37	47	57	67	77	87	97
8	18	28	38	48	58	68	78	88	98
9	19	29	39	49	59	69	79	89	99
10	20	30	40	50	60	70	80	90	100

S

shapes

2-dimensional

3-dimensional

shorter

The crayon is **shorter** than the pencil.

shortest

The paper clip is the **shortest**.

Show All Totals Method

$$
\begin{array}{r}
25 \\
+\ 48 \\
\hline
60 \\
13 \\
\hline
73
\end{array}
$$

side

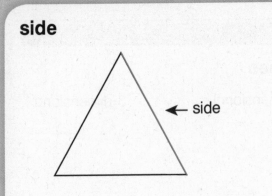

← side

sort

You can **sort** the bugs into groups.

sphere

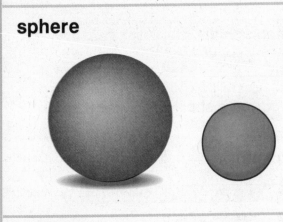

square

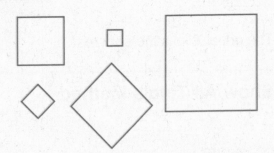

square corner

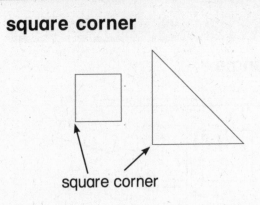

square corner

sticks and circles

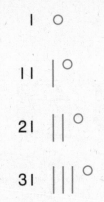

subtract

8 − 3 = 5

subtraction story problem

8 flies are on a log.
6 are eaten by a frog.
How many flies are left?

switch the partners

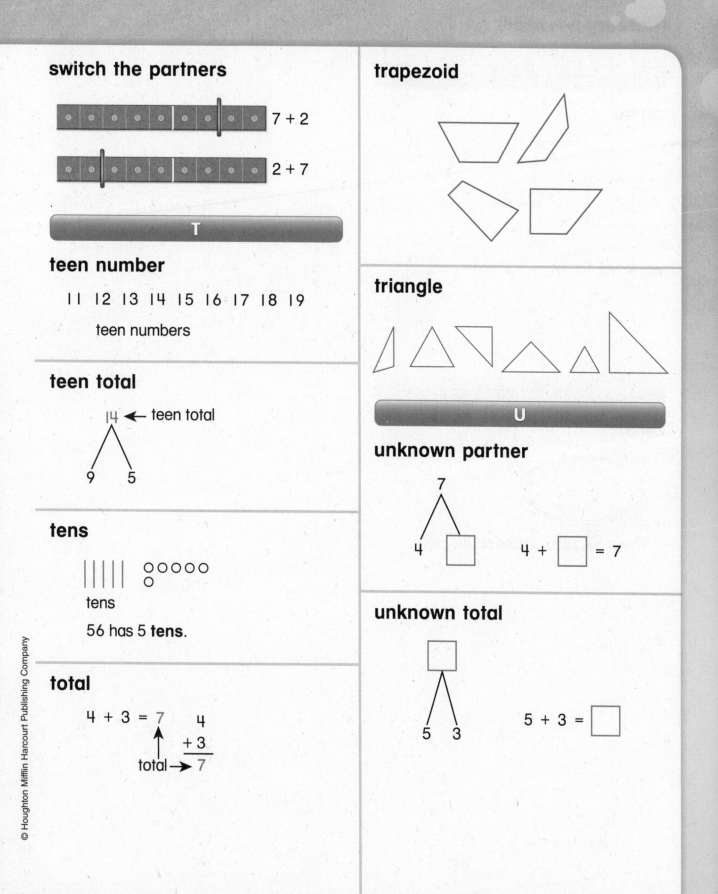

7 + 2

2 + 7

teen number

11 12 13 14 15 16 17 18 19

teen numbers

teen total

14 ← teen total

9   5

tens

||||| ooooo
        o

tens

56 has 5 **tens**.

total

4 + 3 = 7   4
            + 3
total →   7

trapezoid

triangle

unknown partner

7

4   ☐   4 + ☐ = 7

unknown total

☐

5   3   5 + 3 = ☐

© Houghton Mifflin Harcourt Publishing Company

V

vertex

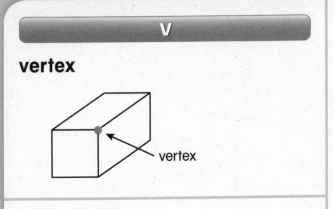

vertex

vertical form

$$\begin{array}{r} 6 \\ +3 \\ \hline 9 \end{array} \qquad \begin{array}{r} 9 \\ -3 \\ \hline 6 \end{array}$$

Z

zero

There are **zero** apples on the plate.

California Common Core Standards for Mathematical Content

1.OA Operations and Algebraic Thinking

Represent and solve problems involving addition and subtraction.

1.OA.1	Use addition and subtraction within 20 to solve word problems involving situations of adding to, taking from, putting together, taking apart, and comparing, with unknowns in all positions, e.g., by using objects, drawings, and equations with a symbol for the unknown number to represent the problem.	Unit 1 Lessons 2, 3, 4, 5, 6, 7, 8; Unit 2 Lessons 1, 2, 3, 4, 10, 11, 12, 13, 14, 15, 16; Unit 3 Lessons 2, 4, 5, 6, 7, 8, 9, 10, 11, 12; Unit 4 Lesson 5; Unit 5 Lessons 1, 2, 3, 4, 5, 11; Unit 6 Lessons 1, 2, 3, 4, 5, 6, 7, 8, 9
1.OA.2	Solve word problems that call for addition of three whole numbers whose sum is less than or equal to 20, e.g., by using objects, drawings, and equations with a symbol for the unknown number to represent the problem.	Unit 5 Lessons 6, 11; Unit 6 Lessons 1, 4, 5, 9

Understand and apply properties of operations and the relationship between addition and subtraction.

1.OA.3	Apply properties of operations as strategies to add and subtract.	Unit 1 Lessons 3, 4, 5, 6, 7, 8, 9; Unit 2 Lesson 7; Unit 4 Lesson 5; Unit 5 Lesson 6
1.OA.4	Understand subtraction as an unknown-addend problem.	Unit 3 Lessons 6, 7, 8, 9, 10, 12; Unit 5 Lessons 1, 2, 5

Add and subtract within 20.

1.OA.5	Relate counting to addition and subtraction (e.g., by counting on 2 to add 2).	Unit 1 Lessons 1, 2, 3, 4, 5, 6, 7, 8, 9; Unit 2 Lessons 5, 6, 7, 8, 9; Unit 3 Lessons 1, 3, 4, 6, 7, 11; Unit 4 Lessons 1, 4, 5, 7, 15, 16; Unit 5 Lessons 1, 2, 4 **Quick Practices:** Five Crows in a Row; Giant Number Cards

1.OA.6	Add and subtract within 20, demonstrating fluency for addition and subtraction within 10. Use strategies such as counting on; making ten (e.g., $8 + 6 = 8 + 2 + 4 = 10 + 4 = 14$); decomposing a number leading to a ten (e.g., $13 - 4 = 13 - 3 - 1 = 10 - 1 = 9$); using the relationship between addition and subtraction (e.g., knowing that $8 + 4 = 12$, one knows $12 - 8 = 4$); and creating equivalent but easier or known sums (e.g., adding $6 + 7$ by creating the known equivalent $6 + 6 + 1 = 12 + 1 = 13$).	Unit 1 Lessons 3, 4, 5, 6, 7, 8, 9; Unit 2 Lessons 1, 2, 3, 5, 6, 7, 8, 9, 10, 11, 12, 14, 15, 16; Unit 3 Lessons 1, 3, 4, 5, 6, 7, 10, 11, 12; Unit 4 Lessons 4, 5, 6, 10, 11, 15; Unit 5 Lessons 1, 2, 3, 4, 5, 10, 11; Unit 6 Lessons 3, 8; Unit 7 Lessons 5, 8, 13; Unit 8 Lesson 5 **Daily Routines:** Number Partners; Partner Houses; Mountains and Equations; Add and Subtract Within 10; Add and Subtract Teen Numbers **Quick Practices:** Doubles to 10; Partners of 10; After or the Same? (+1 or +0); Add and Subtract 0; Count on from the Greater Number; After or Before? (+1 or −1); Before or the Same? (−1 or −0); Count On to Find the Unknown Partner; Count On to Subtract; Add Within 10; Unknown Partners Within 10; Double the Bubbles; Partner Pairs

Work with addition and subtraction equations.

1.OA.7	Understand the meaning of the equal sign, and determine if equations involving addition and subtraction are true or false.	Unit 2 Lessons 1, 2, 3, 4, 11, 12, 13, 16; Unit 3 Lesson 12
1.OA.8	Determine the unknown whole number in an addition or subtraction equation relating three whole numbers.	Unit 1 Lessons 3, 4, 5, 6, 7, 8; Unit 2 Lessons 5, 6, 7, 8, 9, 10, 12, 13, 16; Unit 3 Lessons 3, 4, 6, 7, 9, 11, 12; Unit 4 Lessons 4, 5, 10, 11; Unit 5 Lessons 1, 2, 3, 4, 5

1.NBT Number and Operations in Base Ten

Extend the counting sequence.

1.NBT.1	Count to 120, starting at any number less than 120. In this range, read and write numerals and represent a number of objects with a written numeral.	Unit 4 Lessons 1, 2, 7, 8, 9, 10, 11, 15, 16, 18; Unit 5 Lessons 7, 8, 9 **Daily Routine:** Counting Tens and Ones **Quick Practices:** Count 1–10 on the Number Parade; Number Patterns; Listen for Patterns; Count to 100; One More Tiger, One Less Tiger; Count to 120 Starting at Any Number; Count to 120

Understand place value.

1.NBT.2	Understand that the two digits of a two-digit number represent amounts of tens and ones. Understand the following as special cases:	Unit 4 Lessons 1, 2, 3, 4, 7, 8, 9, 10, 11, 12, 13, 14, 16, 17, 18; Unit 5 Lessons 7, 8, 9 **Daily Routine:** Counting Tens and Ones **Quick Practices:** Show Tens and Ones; Flash Tens and Ones
1.NBT.2a	**a.** 10 can be thought of as a bundle of ten ones — called a "ten."	Unit 4 Lessons 1, 2, 3, 4, 9, 10, 16, 18 **Daily Routine:** Counting Tens and Ones
1.NBT.2b	**b.** The numbers from 11 to 19 are composed of a ten and one, two, three, four, five, six, seven, eight, or nine ones.	Unit 4 Lessons 2, 3, 4, 5, 8, 10 **Quick Practices:** Number Patterns; Teen Number Flashes; Teen Secret Code Cards
1.NBT.2c	**c.** The numbers 10, 20, 30, 40, 50, 60, 70, 80, 90 refer to one, two, three, four, five, six, seven, eight, or nine tens (and 0 ones).	Unit 4 Lessons 1, 7, 8, 9, 13, 14, 18; Unit 5 Lesson 10 **Daily Routine:** Counting Tens and Ones **Quick Practices:** Listen for Patterns; Name the Number
1.NBT.3	Compare two two-digit numbers based on meanings of the tens and ones digits, recording the results of comparisons with the symbols >, =, and <.	Unit 4 Lessons 3, 12, 16, 18; Unit 8 Lesson 6 **Daily Routine:** Greater and Less **Quick Practice:** Compare 2-Digit Numbers

Use place value understanding and properties of operations to add and subtract.

1.NBT.4	Add within 100, including adding a two-digit number and a one-digit number, and adding a two-digit number and a multiple of 10, using concrete models or drawings and strategies based on place value, properties of operations, and/or the relationship between addition and subtraction; relate the strategy to a written method and explain the reasoning used. Understand that in adding two-digit numbers, one adds tens and tens, ones and ones; and sometimes it is necessary to compose a ten.	Unit 4 Lessons 9, 10, 11, 13, 14, 15, 16, 17, 18; Unit 5 Lessons 9, 10, 11; Unit 8 Lessons 1, 2, 3, 4, 5, 6 **Daily Routine:** Counting Tens and Ones **Quick Practices:** The Beetle Rhyme; Partner Pairs
1.NBT.5	Given a two-digit number, mentally find 10 more or 10 less than the number, without having to count; explain the reasoning used.	Unit 4 Lesson 1; Unit 5 Lessons 8, 9 **Quick Practices:** The Lion's Den; The Beetle Rhyme
1.NBT.6	Subtract multiples of 10 in the range 10–90 from multiples of 10 in the range 10–90 (positive or zero differences), using concrete models or drawings and strategies based on place value, properties of operations, and/or the relationship between addition and subtraction; relate the strategy to a written method and explain the reasoning used.	Unit 5 Lessons 9, 10, 11; Unit 8 Lesson 6 **Quick Practice:** Subtract Tens

1.MD Measurement and Data

Measure lengths indirectly and by iterating length units.

1.MD.1	Order three objects by length; compare the lengths of two objects indirectly by using a third object.	Unit 7 Lessons 12, 14
1.MD.2	Express the length of an object as a whole number of length units, by laying multiple copies of a shorter object (the length unit) end to end; understand that the length measurement of an object is the number of same-size length units that span it with no gaps or overlaps.	Unit 7 Lessons 13, 14

Tell and write time.

1.MD.3	Tell and write time in hours and half-hours using analog and digital clocks.	Unit 7 Lessons 1, 2, 3, 4, 5, 14 **Daily Routine:** Telling Time **Quick Practice:** Tell Time

Represent and interpret data.

1.MD.4	Organize, represent, and interpret data with up to three categories; ask and answer questions about the total number of data points, how many in each category, and how many more or less are in one category than in another.	Unit 6 Lessons 1, 2, 3, 4, 5, 9

1.G Geometry

Reason with shapes and their attributes.

1.G.1	Distinguish between defining attributes (e.g. triangles are closed and three-sided) versus non-defining attributes (e.g., color, orientation, overall size); build and draw shapes to possess defining attributes.	Unit 7 Lessons 6, 7, 8, 9, 10, 11
1.G.2	Compose two-dimensional shapes (rectangles, squares, trapezoids, triangles, half-circles, and quarter-circles) or three-dimensional shapes (cubes, right rectangular prisms, right circular cones, and right circular cylinders) to create a composite shape, and compose new shapes from the composite shape.	Unit 7 Lessons 9, 10, 11
1.G.3	Partition circles and rectangles into two and four equal shares, describe the shares using the words *halves*, *fourths*, and *quarters*, and use the phrases *half of*, *fourth of*, and *quarter of*. Describe the whole as two of, or four of the shares. Understand for these examples that decomposing into more equal shares creates smaller shares.	Unit 7 Lessons 8, 9, 14

California Common Core Standards for Mathematical Practice

MP.1 Make sense of problems and persevere in solving them.

Mathematically proficient students start by explaining to themselves the meaning of a problem and looking for entry points to its solution. They analyze givens, constraints, relationships, and goals. They make conjectures about the form and meaning of the solution and plan a solution pathway rather than simply jumping into a solution attempt. They consider analogous problems, and try special cases and simpler forms of the original problem in order to gain insight into its solution. They monitor and evaluate their progress and change course if necessary. Older students might, depending on the context of the problem, transform algebraic expressions or change the viewing window on their graphing calculator to get the information they need. Mathematically proficient students can explain correspondences between equations, verbal descriptions, tables, and graphs or draw diagrams of important features and relationships, graph data, and search for regularity or trends. Younger students might rely on using concrete objects or pictures to help conceptualize and solve a problem. Mathematically proficient students check their answers to problems using a different method, and they continually ask themselves, "Does this make sense?" They can understand the approaches of others to solving complex problems and identify correspondences between different approaches.

Unit 1 Lessons 2, 3, 4, 6, 8, 9

Unit 2 Lessons 1, 2, 3, 4, 6, 7, 8, 9, 10, 13, 14, 16

Unit 3 Lessons 1, 2, 3, 4, 6, 7, 8, 9, 10, 11, 12

Unit 4 Lessons 2, 3, 5, 10, 18

Unit 5 Lessons 1, 2, 3, 4, 5, 6, 11

Unit 6 Lessons 1, 2, 4, 6, 7, 8, 9

Unit 7 Lessons 8, 14

Unit 8 Lessons 1, 3, 4, 6

MP.2 Reason abstractly and quantitatively.

Mathematically proficient students make sense of quantities and their relationships in problem situations. They bring two complementary abilities to bear on problems involving quantitative relationships: the ability to *decontextualize*—to abstract a given situation and represent it symbolically and manipulate the representing symbols as if they have a life of their own, without necessarily attending to their referents—and the ability to *contextualize*, to pause as needed during the manipulation process in order to probe into the referents for the symbols involved. Quantitative reasoning entails habits of creating a coherent representation of the problem at hand; considering the units involved; attending to the meaning of quantities, not just how to compute them; and knowing and flexibly using different properties of operations and objects.

Unit 1 Lessons 3, 4, 5, 6, 7, 8, 9

Unit 2 Lessons 1, 2, 3, 4, 6, 10, 11, 12, 13, 15, 16

Unit 3 Lessons 3, 5, 6, 12

Unit 4 Lessons 1, 2, 3, 4, 6, 7, 8, 9, 10, 11, 12, 14, 15, 16, 18

Unit 5 Lessons 1, 2, 3, 4, 5, 9, 10, 11

Unit 6 Lessons 1, 2, 3, 5, 6, 8, 9

Unit 7 Lessons 8, 9, 14

Unit 8 Lessons 1, 2, 3, 4, 5, 6

MP.3 Construct viable arguments and critique the reasoning of others.

Mathematically proficient students understand and use stated assumptions, definitions, and previously established results in constructing arguments. They make conjectures and build a logical progression of statements to explore the truth of their conjectures. They are able to analyze situations by breaking them into cases, and can recognize and use counterexamples. They justify their conclusions, communicate them to others, and respond to the arguments of others. They reason inductively about data, making plausible arguments that take into account the context from which the data arose. Mathematically proficient students are also able to compare the effectiveness of two plausible arguments, distinguish correct logic or reasoning from that which is flawed, and—if there is a flaw in an argument—explain what it is. Elementary students can construct arguments using concrete referents such as objects, drawings, diagrams, and actions. Such arguments can make sense and be correct, even though they are not generalized or made formal until later grades. Later, students learn to determine domains to which an argument applies. Students at all grades can listen or read the arguments of others, decide whether they make sense, and ask useful questions to clarify or improve the arguments.

Unit 1 Lessons 1, 2, 3, 4, 5, 6, 7, 8, 9

Unit 2 Lessons 1, 2, 3, 4, 5, 6, 7, 8, 9, 10, 11, 12, 13, 14, 15, 16

Unit 3 Lessons 1, 2, 3, 4, 5, 6, 7, 8, 9, 10, 11, 12

Unit 4 Lessons 1, 2, 3, 4, 5, 6, 7, 8, 9, 10, 11, 12, 13, 14, 15, 16, 17, 18

Unit 5 Lessons 1, 2, 3, 4, 5, 6, 7, 8, 9, 10, 11

Unit 6 Lessons 1, 2, 3, 4, 5, 6, 7, 8, 9

Unit 7 Lessons 1, 2, 3, 4, 5, 6, 7, 8, 9, 10, 11, 12, 13, 14

Unit 8 Lessons 1, 2, 3, 4, 5, 6

MP.4 Model with mathematics.

Mathematically proficient students can apply the mathematics they know to solve problems arising in everyday life, society, and the workplace. In early grades, this might be as simple as writing an addition equation to describe a situation. In middle grades, a student might apply proportional reasoning to plan a school event or analyze a problem in the community. By high school, a student might use geometry to solve a design problem or use a function to describe how one quantity of interest depends on another. Mathematically proficient students who can apply what they know are comfortable making assumptions and approximations to simplify a complicated situation, realizing that these may need revision later. They are able to identify important quantities in a practical situation and map their relationships using such tools as diagrams, two-way tables, graphs, flowcharts and formulas. They can analyze those relationships mathematically to draw conclusions. They routinely interpret their mathematical results in the context of the situation and reflect on whether the results make sense, possibly improving the model if it has not served its purpose.

Unit 1 Lessons 2, 3, 9

Unit 2 Lessons 1, 2, 10, 13, 16

Unit 3 Lessons 1, 2, 5, 6, 7, 8, 9, 10, 11, 12

Unit 4 Lessons 3, 5, 10, 18

Unit 5 Lessons 1, 2, 3, 4, 6, 11

Unit 6 Lessons 2, 3, 4, 5, 6, 7, 8, 9

Unit 7 Lessons 3, 8, 14

Unit 8 Lessons 1, 2, 3, 6

MP.5 Use appropriate tools strategically.

Mathematically proficient students consider the available tools when solving a mathematical problem. These tools might include pencil and paper, concrete models, a ruler, a protractor, a calculator, a spreadsheet, a computer algebra system, a statistical package, or dynamic geometry software. Proficient students are sufficiently familiar with tools appropriate for their grade or course to make sound decisions about when each of these tools might be helpful, recognizing both the insight to be gained and their limitations. For example, mathematically proficient high school students analyze graphs of functions and solutions generated using a graphing calculator. They detect possible errors by strategically using estimation and other mathematical knowledge. When making mathematical models, they know that technology can enable them to visualize the results of varying assumptions, explore consequences, and compare predictions with data. Mathematically proficient students at various grade levels are able to identify relevant external mathematical resources, such as digital content located on a website, and use them to pose or solve problems. They are able to use technological tools to explore and deepen their understanding of concepts.

Unit 1 Lessons 1, 2, 3, 4, 5, 6, 7, 8, 9

Unit 2 Lessons 5, 6, 8, 16

Unit 3 Lessons 1, 2, 3, 4, 7, 11, 12

Unit 4 Lessons 1, 2, 3, 4, 5, 6, 7, 8, 9, 10, 11, 12, 13, 14, 16, 17, 18

Unit 5 Lessons 1, 2, 6, 7, 8, 9, 10, 11

Unit 6 Lessons 3, 5, 8, 9

Unit 7 Lessons 1, 2, 5, 6, 7, 8, 9, 10, 11, 12, 13, 14

Unit 8 Lessons 2, 3, 6

MP.6 Attend to precision.

Mathematically proficient students try to communicate precisely to others. They try to use clear definitions in discussion with others and in their own reasoning. They state the meaning of the symbols they choose, including using the equal sign consistently and appropriately. They are careful about specifying units of measure, and labeling axes to clarify the correspondence with quantities in a problem. They calculate accurately and efficiently, express numerical answers with a degree of precision appropriate for the problem context. In the elementary grades, students give carefully formulated explanations to each other. By the time they reach high school they have learned to examine claims and make explicit use of definitions.

Unit 1 Lessons 1, 2, 3, 4, 5, 6, 7, 8, 9

Unit 2 Lessons 1, 2, 3, 4, 5, 6, 7, 8, 9, 10, 11, 12, 13, 14, 15, 16

Unit 3 Lessons 1, 2, 3, 4, 5, 6, 7, 8, 9, 10, 11, 12

Unit 4 Lessons 1, 2, 3, 4, 5, 6, 7, 8, 9, 10, 11, 12, 13, 14, 15, 16, 17, 18

Unit 5 Lessons 1, 2, 3, 4, 5, 6, 7, 8, 9, 10, 11

Unit 6 Lessons 1, 2, 3, 4, 5, 6, 7, 8, 9

Unit 7 Lessons 1, 2, 3, 4, 5, 6, 7, 8, 9, 10, 11, 12, 13, 14

Unit 8 Lessons 1, 2, 3, 4, 5, 6

MP.7 Look for and make use of structure.

Mathematically proficient students look closely to discern a pattern or structure. Young students, for example, might notice that three and seven more is the same amount as seven and three more, or they may sort a collection of shapes according to how many sides the shapes have. Later, students will see 7×8 equals the well remembered $7 \times 5 + 7 \times 3$, in preparation for learning about the distributive property. In the expression $x^2 + 9x + 14$, older students can see the 14 as 2×7 and the 9 as $2 + 7$. They recognize the significance of an existing line in a geometric figure and can use the strategy of drawing an auxiliary line for solving problems. They also can step back for an overview and shift perspective. They can see complicated things, such as some algebraic expressions, as single objects or as being composed of several objects. For example, they can see $5 - 3(x - y)^2$ as 5 minus a positive number times a square and use that to realize that its value cannot be more than 5 for any real numbers x and y.

Unit 1 Lessons 1, 2, 3, 4, 5, 6, 7, 8, 9

Unit 2 Lessons 13, 14, 16

Unit 3 Lessons 1, 3, 9, 12

Unit 4 Lessons 1, 2, 3, 5, 6, 7, 8, 9, 10, 13, 17, 18

Unit 5 Lessons 1, 2, 3, 5, 6, 7, 8, 9, 10, 11

Unit 6 Lessons 6, 8, 9

Unit 7 Lessons 1, 2, 3, 4, 5, 6, 7, 9, 10, 11, 14

Unit 8 Lesson 6

MP.8 Look for and express regularity in repeated reasoning.

Mathematically proficient students notice if calculations are repeated, and look both for general methods and for shortcuts. Upper elementary students might notice when dividing 25 by 11 that they are repeating the same calculations over and over again, and conclude they have a repeating decimal. By paying attention to the calculation of slope as they repeatedly check whether points are on the line through (1, 2) with slope 3, middle school students might abstract the equation $(y - 2)/(x - 1) = 3$. Noticing the regularity in the way terms cancel when expanding $(x - 1)(x + 1)$, $(x - 1)(x^2 + x + 1)$, and $(x - 1)(x^3 + x^2 + x + 1)$ might lead them to the general formula for the sum of a geometric series. As they work to solve a problem, mathematically proficient students maintain oversight of the process, while attending to the details. They continually evaluate the reasonableness of their intermediate results.

Unit 1 Lessons 1, 2, 3, 4, 5, 6, 7, 8, 9

Unit 2 Lessons 6, 7, 8, 11, 14, 16

Unit 3 Lessons 8, 9, 12

Unit 4 Lessons 1, 2, 5, 6, 7, 9, 10, 12, 13, 14, 15, 17, 18

Unit 5 Lessons 1, 2, 4, 5, 6, 7, 8, 9, 10, 11

Unit 6 Lessons 1, 6, 7, 9

Unit 7 Lessons 3, 6, 7, 8, 9, 10, 12, 14

Unit 8 Lessons 1, 2, 4, 6

Index

© Houghton Mifflin Harcourt Publishing Company

B

C

Triangle Grid, 227

Two-Dimensional Shape Set,
    213–214, 215–216, 226, 228

Math Mountains, 13, 15, 17, 19, 21,
34, 67–68, 85–86, 187

Measurement

length
    iterate, 235–236, 238
    order, 233–234, 238
    units, 235–236, 238

time
    analog clock, 203–204, 207–208,
        209–210, 211–212
    digital clock, 203–204, 207–208,
        209–210, 211–212
    half-hour, 209–210, 211–212
    hour, 203–204, 207–208, 212

N

New Group Above method,
247–248, 249

New Group Below method, 247–248,
249

Number-Bond diagram. See Math
Mountains.

Number Cards, 7–8

Number Quilt, 47–48, 75–76, 91–92

Numbers

5-groups, 23

decade, 101, 115–116,
    123–124, 165

doubles, 16, 19–20, 24, 113–114

number words, 115–116

read and write, 25, 115–116,
    129–130, 161–162

represent, 13, 15, 17, 19, 21, 23, 26,
    101–102, 105, 117, 129–130

teen, 105–106, 111–112, 113–114,
    115–116, 141–142, 147–148,
    149–150, 151–152, 153–154

to 10, 13–14, 15–16, 17–18, 19–20,
    21–22, 23–24, 25–26

to 100, 101–102, 115–116, 117,
    129–130, 157–158

two-digit, 101–102, 115–116

zero, 14, 16, 20, 24

P

Partners. See also Break-Aparts;
Math Mountains.

of 2, 13–14, 16

of 3, 13–14, 16, 18, 20, 22, 24

of 4, 13–14, 16, 18, 20, 22, 24

of 5, 13–14, 16, 18, 20, 22, 24

of 6, 15–16, 18, 20, 22, 24

of 7, 17–18, 20, 22, 24

of 8, 19–20, 22, 24

of 9, 21–22, 24

of 10, 23–24, 26

switch, 17–18, 19, 21, 23, 26,
    43–44, 155. See also Addition,
    Commutative Property.

train, 15, 17, 19, 21

unknown, 67–68, 70, 71, 85–86, 141

zero as a partner, 14, 16, 20, 24

© Houghton Mifflin Harcourt Publishing Company

Subtraction

equation, 51–52, 53–54, 55–56, 147
  determine the unknown whole
    number, 80, 83–84, 86, 90,
    93–94, 147–148, 149–150,
    154, 165–166
  represent an unknown in, 86, 47
  true and false, 166

fluency practice, 56, 58, 80, 90, 114,
  152, 166, 190, 224

model
  comparison bars, 185–186,
    187–188, 189–190
  drawings
    circle, 53–54, 55–56, 57
    ten-stick and circles, 164, 166
  equations, 86, 90, 148, 164,
    166, 168
  Math Mountains, 83, 86, 87–88,
    187

minus sign, 51–52

multiples of ten. *See* Two-digit
  numbers, subtraction.

relate to addition, 57–58, 85–86

situation and solution equations,
  85–86, 187

story problems. *See also* Problem
  Types.
  solve with drawings, 55–56, 79, 84,
    87–88
  solve with equations, 51, 53–54,
    55–56, 57, 59, 80, 86
  solve with objects, 93–94, 148, 164

strategies
  decompose a number leading to
    a ten, 148
  make a ten, 147

patterns, 16, 18, 20, 24
relate addition and subtraction,
  57–58, 85–86
understand subtraction as an
  unknown addend problem, 57,
  83–84, 86, 93

within 10, 24, 51–52, 53–54, 55–56,
  57–58, 59, 79–80, 83–84, 86,
  87–88, 90, 93–94

within 20, 147–148, 149–150,
  151–152, 153–154, 168

Symbols

equal (=), 37–38
inequality (<, >), 121–122
minus (−), 51–52
plus (+), 13–14, 33–34

T

Tape diagrams. *See* Comparison bars.

Teen Numbers, 105–106, 111–112,
115–116, 141–142, 147–148,
149–150, 151–152, 153–154

Three-dimensional shapes, 229–230,
231–232. *See* Geometry.

Time

analog clock, 203–204, 207–208,
  209–210, 211–212
digital clock, 203–204, 207–208,
  209–210, 211–212
half-hour, 209–210, 211–212
hour, 203–204, 207–208, 212

Triangle, 219–220, 226

Triangle Grid, 227

© Houghton Mifflin Harcourt Publishing Company

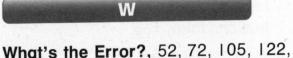